THE PELICAN SHAKESPEARE
GENERAL EDITORS

STEPHEN ORGEL
A. R. BRAUNMULLER

The Life of King Henry the Eighth

Ellen Terry as a bravura Queen Katherine at the Lyceum
Theatre, London, 1892. Cardinal Wolsey was played by
Henry Irving, the king by William Terriss; in the small role
of Thomas Cromwell appeared the nineteen-year-old Edward
Gordon Craig, Ellen Terry's son, who subsequently became
one of the great modern stage designers. From a sketch
by J. Bernard Partridge in the souvenir program.

# William Shakespeare

---

# The Life of King Henry
# the Eighth

EDITED BY JONATHAN CREWE

PENGUIN BOOKS

PENGUIN BOOKS
Published by the Penguin Group
Penguin Putnam Inc., 375 Hudson Street,
New York, New York 10014, U.S.A.
Penguin Books Ltd, 27 Wrights Lane, London W8 5TZ, England
Penguin Books Australia Ltd, Ringwood, Victoria, Australia
Penguin Books Canada Ltd, 10 Alcorn Avenue,
Toronto, Ontario, Canada M4V 3B2
Penguin Books (N.Z.) Ltd, 182–190 Wairau Road,
Auckland 10, New Zealand

Penguin Books Ltd, Registered Offices:
Harmondsworth, Middlesex, England

*The Life of King Henry the Eighth* edited by F. David Hoeniger
published in the United States of America in Penguin Books 1966
Revised edition published 1981
This new edition edited by Jonathan Crewe published 2001

5   7   9   10   8   6   4

LIBRARY OF CONGRESS CATALOGING IN PUBLICATION DATA
Shakespeare, William, 1564–1616.
[King Henry VIII]
Henry VIII / William Shakespeare; edited by Jonathan Crewe.
p.   cm. – (The Pelican Shakespeare)
ISBN 0 14 07.1475 8 (pbk. : alk. paper)
1. Henry VIII, King of England, 1491–1547 – Drama.   2. Great
Britain – History – Henry VIII, 1509–1547 – Drama.   I. Crewe,
Jonathan V. II. Title.   III. Series.
PR2817.A2 C74 2001
822.3'3 – dc21          2001031338

Printed in the United States of America
Set in Adobe Garamond
Designed by Virginia Norey

# Contents

# Publisher's Note

IT IS ALMOST half a century since the first volumes of the Pelican Shakespeare appeared under the general editorship of Alfred Harbage. The fact that a new edition, rather than simply a revision, has been undertaken reflects the profound changes textual and critical studies of Shakespeare have undergone in the past twenty years. For the new Pelican series, the texts of the plays and poems have been thoroughly revised in accordance with recent scholarship, and in some cases have been entirely reedited. New introductions and notes have been provided in all the volumes. But the new Shakespeare is also designed as a successor to the original series; the previous editions have been taken into account, and the advice of the previous editors has been solicited where it was feasible to do so.

Certain textual features of the new Pelican Shakespeare should be particularly noted. All lines are numbered that contain a word, phrase, or allusion explained in the glossarial notes. In addition, for convenience, every tenth line is also numbered, in italics when no annotation is indicated. The intrusive and often inaccurate place headings inserted by early editors are omitted (as is becoming standard practice), but for the convenience of those who miss them, an indication of locale now appears as the first item in the annotation of each scene.

In the interest of both elegance and utility, each speech prefix is set in a separate line when the speaker's lines are in verse, except when those words form the second half of a verse line. Thus the verse form of the speech is kept visually intact. What is printed as verse and what is printed as prose has, in general, the authority of the original texts. Departures from the original texts in this regard have only the authority of editorial tradition and the judgment of the Pelican editors; and, in a few instances, are admittedly arbitrary.

# The Theatrical World

ECONOMIC REALITIES determined the theatrical world in which Shakespeare's plays were written, performed, and received. For centuries in England, the primary theatrical tradition was nonprofessional. Craft guilds (or "mysteries") provided religious drama – mystery plays – as part of the celebration of religious and civic festivals, and schools and universities staged classical and neoclassical drama in both Latin and English as part of their curricula. In these forms, drama was established and socially acceptable. Professional theater, in contrast, existed on the margins of society. The acting companies were itinerant; playhouses could be any available space – the great halls of the aristocracy, town squares, civic halls, inn yards, fair booths, or open fields – and income was sporadic, dependent on the passing of the hat or on the bounty of local patrons. The actors, moreover, were considered little better than vagabonds, constantly in danger of arrest or expulsion.

In the late 1560s and 1570s, however, English professional theater began to gain respectability. Wealthy aristocrats fond of drama – the Lord Admiral, for example, or the Lord Chamberlain – took acting companies under their protection so that the players technically became members of their households and were no longer subject to arrest as homeless or masterless men. Permanent theaters were first built at this time as well, allowing the companies to control and charge for entry to their performances.

Shakespeare's livelihood, and the stunning artistic explosion in which he participated, depended on pragmatic and architectural effort. Professional theater requires ways to restrict access to its offerings; if it does not, and admission fees cannot be charged, the actors do not get paid, the costumes go to a pawnbroker, and there is no such thing as a professional, ongoing theatrical tradition. The answer to that economic need arrived in the late 1560s and 1570s with the creation of the so-called public or amphitheater playhouse. Recent discoveries indicate that the precursor of the Globe playhouse in London (where Shakespeare's mature plays were presented) and the Rose theater (which presented Christopher Marlowe's plays and some of Shakespeare's earliest ones) was the Red Lion theater of 1567. Archaeological studies of the foundations of the Rose and Globe theaters have revealed that the open-air theater of the 1590s and later was probably a polygonal building with fourteen to twenty or twenty-four sides, multistoried, from 75 to 100 feet in diameter, with a raised, partly covered "thrust" stage that projected into a group of standing patrons, or "groundlings," and a covered gallery, seating up to 2,500 or more (very crowded) spectators.

These theaters might have been about half full on any given day, though the audiences were larger on holidays or when a play was advertised, as old and new were, through printed playbills posted around London. The metropolitan area's late-Tudor, early-Stuart population (circa 1590–1620) has been estimated at about 150,000 to 250,000. It has been supposed that in the mid-1590s there were about 15,000 spectators per week at the public theaters; thus, as many as 10 percent of the local population went to the theater regularly. Consequently, the theaters' repertories – the plays available for this experienced and frequent audience – had to change often: in the month between September 15 and October 15, 1595, for instance, the Lord Admiral's Men performed twenty-eight times in eighteen different plays.

Since natural light illuminated the amphitheaters' stages, performances began between noon and two o'clock and ran without a break for two or three hours. They often concluded with a jig, a fencing display, or some other nondramatic exhibition. Weather conditions determined the season for the amphitheaters: plays were performed every day (including Sundays, sometimes, to clerical dismay) except during Lent – the forty days before Easter – or periods of plague, or sometimes during the summer months when law courts were not in session and the most affluent members of the audience were not in London.

To a modern theatergoer, an amphitheater stage like that of the Rose or Globe would appear an unfamiliar mixture of plainness and elaborate decoration. Much of the structure was carved or painted, sometimes to imitate marble; elsewhere, as under the canopy projecting over the stage, to represent the stars and the zodiac. Appropriate painted canvas pictures (of Jerusalem, for example, if the play was set in that city) were apparently hung on the wall behind the acting area, and tragedies were accompanied by black hangings, presumably something like crepe festoons or bunting. Although these theaters did not employ what we would call scenery, early modern spectators saw numerous large props, such as the "bar" at which a prisoner stood during a trial, the "mossy bank" where lovers reclined, an arbor for amorous conversation, a chariot, gallows, tables, trees, beds, thrones, writing desks, and so forth. Audiences might learn a scene's location from a sign (reading "Athens," for example) carried across the stage (as in Bertolt Brecht's twentieth-century productions). Equally captivating (and equally irritating to the theater's enemies) were the rich costumes and personal props the actors used: the most valuable items in the surviving theatrical inventories are the swords, gowns, robes, crowns, and other items worn or carried by the performers.

Magic appealed to Shakespeare's audiences as much as it does to us today, and the theater exploited many deceptive and spectacular devices. A winch in the loft above the stage, called "the heavens," could lower and raise actors playing gods, goddesses, and other supernatural figures to and from the main acting area, just as one or more trap-doors permitted entrances and exits to and from the area, called "hell," beneath the stage. Actors wore elementary makeup such as wigs, false beards, and face paint, and they employed pig's bladders filled with animal blood to make wounds seem more real. They had rudimentary but effective ways of pretending to behead or hang a person. Supernumeraries (stagehands or actors not needed in a particular scene) could make thunder sounds (by shaking a metal sheet or rolling an iron ball down a chute) and show lightning (by blowing inflammable resin through tubes into a flame). Elaborate fireworks enhanced the ef-fects of dragons flying through the air or imitated such ce-lestial phenomena as comets, shooting stars, and multiple suns. Horses' hoofbeats, bells (located perhaps in the tower above the stage), trumpets and drums, clocks, can-non shots and gunshots, and the like were common sound effects. And the music of viols, cornets, oboes, and recorders was a regular feature of theatrical performances.

For two relatively brief spans, from the late 1570s to 1590 and from 1599 to 1614, the amphitheaters com-peted with the so-called private, or indoor, theaters, which originated as, or later represented themselves as, educational institutions training boys as singers for church services and court performances. These indoor theaters had two features that were distinct from the am-phitheaters': their personnel and their playing spaces. The amphitheaters' adult companies included both adult men, who played the male roles, and boys, who played the female roles; the private, or indoor, theater companies, on the other hand, were entirely composed of boys aged about 8 to 16, who were, or could pretend to be, can-didates for singers in a church or a royal boys' choir. (Until 1660, professional theatrical companies included no women.) The playing space would appear much more familiar to modern audiences than the long-vanished amphitheaters; the later indoor theaters were, in fact, the ancestors of the typical modern theater. They were enclosed spaces, usually rectangular, with the stage filling one end of the rectangle and the audience arrayed in seats or benches across (and sometimes lining) the building's longer axis. These spaces staged plays less frequently than the public theaters (perhaps only once a week) and held far fewer spectators than the amphitheaters: about 200 to 600, as opposed to 2,500 or more. Fewer patrons mean a smaller gross income, unless each pays more. Not surprisingly, then, private theaters charged higher prices than the amphitheaters, probably sixpence, as opposed to a penny for the cheapest entry.

Protected from the weather, the indoor theaters presented plays later in the day than the amphitheaters, and used artificial illumination – candles in sconces or candelabra. But candles melt, and need replacing, snuffing, and trimming, and these practical requirements may have been part of the reason the indoor theaters introduced breaks in the performance, the intermission so dear to the heart of theatergoers and to the pocketbooks of theater concessionaires ever since. Whether motivated by the need to tend to the candles or by the entrepreneurs' wishing to sell oranges and liquor, or both, the indoor theaters eventually established the modern convention of the non-continuous performance. In the early modern "private" theater, musical performances apparently filled the intermissions, which in Stuart theater jargon seem to have been called "acts."

At the end of the first decade of the seventeenth century, the distinction between public amphitheaters and private indoor companies ceased. For various cultural, political, and economic reasons, individual companies gained control of both the public, open-air theaters and the indoor ones, and companies mixing adult men and boys took over the formerly "private" theaters. Despite the death of the boys' companies and of their highly innova-

tive theaters (for which such luminous playwrights as
Ben Jonson, George Chapman, and John Marston wrote),
their playing spaces and conventions had an immense impact on subsequent plays: not merely for the intervals
(which stressed the artistic and architectonic importance
of "acts"), but also because they introduced political and
social satire as a popular dramatic ingredient, even in
tragedy, and a wider range of actorly effects, encouraged
by their more intimate playing spaces.

Even the briefest sketch of the Shakespearean theatrical
world would be incomplete without some comment on
the social and cultural dimensions of theaters and playing
in the period. In an intensely hierarchical and status-
conscious society, professional actors and their ventures had
hardly any respectability; as we have indicated, to protect
themselves against laws designed to curb vagabondage and
the increase of masterless men, actors resorted to the near-
fiction that they were the servants of noble masters, and
wore their distinctive livery. Hence the company for which
Shakespeare wrote in the 1590s called itself the Lord
Chamberlain's Men and pretended that the public, money-
getting performances were in fact rehearsals for private performances before that high court official. From 1598, the
Privy Council had licensed theatrical companies, and after
1603, with the accession of King James I, the companies
gained explicit royal protection, just as the Queen's Men
had for a time under Queen Elizabeth. The Chamberlain's
Men became the King's Men, and the other companies
were patronized by the other members of the royal family.

These designations were legal fictions that half-
concealed an important economic and social development, the evolution away from the theater's organization
on the model of the guild, a self-regulating confraternity
of individual artisans, into a proto-capitalist organization.
Shakespeare's company became a joint-stock company,
where persons who supplied capital and, in some cases,

such as Shakespeare's, capital and talent, employed themselves and others in earning a return on that capital. This
development meant that actors and theater companies
were outside both the traditional guild structures, which
required some form of civic or royal charter, and the feu-
dal household organization of master-and-servant. This
anomalous, maverick social and economic condition
made theater companies practically unruly and potentially even dangerous; consequently, numerous official
bodies – including the London metropolitan and ecclesi-
astical authorities as well as, occasionally, the royal court
itself – tried, without much success, to control and even
to disband them.

Public officials had good reason to want to close the
theaters: they were attractive nuisances – they drew often
riotous crowds, they were always noisy, and they could be
politically offensive and socially insubordinate. Until the
Civil War, however, anti-theatrical forces failed to shut
down professional theater, for many reasons – limited
surveillance and few police powers, tensions or outright
hostilities among the agencies that sought to check or
channel theatrical activity, and lack of clear policies for
control. Another reason must have been the theaters' un-
deniable popularity. Curtailing any activity enjoyed by
such a substantial percentage of the population was diffi-
cult, as various Roman emperors attempting to limit cir-
cuses had learned, and the Tudor-Stuart audience was not
merely large, it was socially diverse and included women.
The prevalence of public entertainment in this period
has been underestimated. In fact, fairs, holidays, games,
sporting events, the equivalent of modern parades, freak
shows, and street exhibitions all abounded, but the theater was the most widely and frequently available entertainment to which people of every class had access. That
fact helps account both for its quantity and for the fear
and anger it aroused.

## WILLIAM SHAKESPEARE OF
## STRATFORD-UPON-AVON, GENTLEMAN

Many people have said that we know very little about William Shakespeare's life – pinheads and postcards are often mentioned as appropriately tiny surfaces on which to record the available information. More imaginatively and perhaps more correctly, Ralph Waldo Emerson wrote, "Shakespeare is the only biographer of Shakespeare. . . . So far from Shakespeare's being the least known, he is the one person in all modern history fully known to us."

In fact, we know more about Shakespeare's life than we do about almost any other English writer's of his era. His last will and testament (dated March 25, 1616) survives, as do numerous legal contracts and court documents involving Shakespeare as principal or witness, and parish records in Stratford and London. Shakespeare appears quite often in official records of King James's royal court, and of course Shakespeare's name appears on numerous title pages and in the written and recorded words of his literary contemporaries Robert Greene, Henry Chettle, Francis Meres, John Davies of Hereford, Ben Jonson, and many others. Indeed, if we make due allowance for the bloating of modern, run-of-the-mill bureaucratic records, more information has survived over the past four hundred years about William Shakespeare of Stratford-upon-Avon, Warwickshire, than is likely to survive in the next four hundred years about any reader of these words.

What we do not have are entire categories of information – Shakespeare's private letters or diaries, drafts and revisions of poems and plays, critical prefaces or essays, commendatory verse for other writers' works, or instructions guiding his fellow actors in their performances, for instance – that we imagine would help us understand and appreciate his surviving writings. For all we know, many such data never existed as written records. Many literary and theatrical critics, not knowing what might once have existed, more or less cheerfully accept the situation; some even make a theoretical virtue of it by claiming that such data are irrelevant to understanding and interpreting the plays and poems.

So, what do we know about William Shakespeare, the man responsible for thirty-seven or perhaps more plays, more than 150 sonnets, two lengthy narrative poems, and some shorter poems?

While many families by the name of Shakespeare (or some variant spelling) can be identified in the English Midlands as far back as the twelfth century, it seems likely that the dramatist's grandfather, Richard, moved to Snitterfield, a town not far from Stratford-upon-Avon, sometime before 1529. In Snitterfield, Richard Shakespeare leased farmland from the very wealthy Robert Arden. By 1552, Richard's son John had moved to a large house on Henley Street in Stratford-upon-Avon, the house that stands today as "The Birthplace." In Stratford, John Shakespeare traded as a glover, dealt in wool, and lent money at interest; he also served in a variety of civic posts, including "High Bailiff," the municipality's equivalent of mayor. In 1557, he married Robert Arden's youngest daughter, Mary. Mary and John had four sons – William was the oldest – and four daughters, of whom only Joan outlived her most celebrated sibling. William was baptized (an event entered in the Stratford parish church records) on April 26, 1564, and it has become customary, without any good factual support, to suppose he was born on April 23, which happens to be the feast day of Saint George, patron saint of England, and is also the date on which he died, in 1616. Shakespeare married Anne Hathaway in 1582, when he was eighteen and she was twenty-six; their first child was born five months later. It has been generally assumed that the marriage was enforced and subsequently unhappy, but these are only assumptions; it has been estimated, for instance, that up to one third of Elizabethan brides were pregnant when they married. Anne and William Shakespeare had three children: Susanna, who married a prominent local physician, John Hall; and the twins Hamnet, who died young in 1596, and Judith, who married Thomas Quiney – apparently a rather shady individual. The name Hamnet was unusual but not unique: he and his twin sister were named for their godparents, Shakespeare's neighbors Hamnet and Judith Sadler. Shakespeare's father died in 1601 (the year of *Hamlet*), and Mary Arden Shakespeare died in 1608 (the year of *Coriolanus*). William Shakespeare's last surviving direct descendant was his granddaughter Elizabeth Hall, who died in 1670.

Between the birth of the twins in 1585 and a clear reference to Shakespeare as a practicing London dramatist in Robert Greene's sensationalizing, satiric pamphlet, *Greene's Groatsworth of Wit* (1592), there is no record of where William Shakespeare was or what he was doing. These seven so-called lost years have been imaginatively filled by scholars and other students of Shakespeare: some think he traveled to Italy, or fought in the Low Countries, or studied law or medicine, or worked as an apprentice actor/writer, and so on to even more fanciful possibilities. Whatever the biographical facts for those "lost" years, Greene's nasty remarks in 1592 testify to professional envy and to the fact that Shakespeare already had a successful career in London. Speaking to his fellow playwrights, Greene warns both generally and specifically:

> . . . trust them [actors] not: for there is an upstart crow, beautified with our feathers, that with his tiger's heart wrapped in a player's hide supposes he is as well able to bombast out a blank verse as the best of you; and being an absolute Johannes Factotum, is in his own conceit the only Shake-scene in a country.

The passage mimics a line from *3 Henry VI* (hence the play must have been performed before Greene wrote) and seems to say that "Shake-scene" is both actor and play-wright, a jack-of-all-trades. That same year, Henry Chettle protested Greene's remarks in *Kind-Heart's Dream,* and each of the next two years saw the publication of poems – *Venus and Adonis* and *The Rape of Lucrece,* respectively – publicly ascribed to (and dedicated by) Shakespeare. Early in 1595 he was named one of the senior members of a prominent acting company, the Lord Chamberlain's Men, when they received payment for court performances during the 1594 Christmas season.

Clearly, Shakespeare had achieved both success and reputation in London. In 1596, upon Shakespeare's application, the College of Arms granted his father the now-familiar coat of arms he had taken the first steps to obtain almost twenty years before, and in 1598, John's son – now permitted to call himself "gentleman" – took a 10 percent share in the new Globe playhouse. In 1597, he bought a substantial bourgeois house, called New Place, in Stratford – the garden remains, but Shakespeare's house, several times rebuilt, was torn down in 1759 – and over the next few years Shakespeare spent large sums buying land and making other investments in the town and its environs. Though he worked in London, his family remained in Stratford, and he seems always to have considered Stratford the home he would eventually return to. Something approaching a disinterested appreciation of Shakespeare's popular and professional status appears in Francis Meres's *Palladis Tamia* (1598), a not especially imaginative and perhaps therefore persuasive record of literary reputations. Reviewing contemporary English writers, Meres lists the titles of many of Shakespeare's plays, including one not now known, *Love's Labor's Won,* and praises his "mellifluous & hony-tongued" "sugred Sonnets," which were then circulating in manuscript (they were first collected in 1609). Meres describes Shakespeare as "one of the best" English playwrights of both comedy and tragedy. In *Remains . . . Concerning Britain* (1605),

William Camden – a more authoritative source than the imitative Meres – calls Shakespeare one of the "most pregnant witts of these our times" and joins him with such writers as Chapman, Daniel, Jonson, Marston, and Spenser. During the first decades of the seventeenth century, publishers began to attribute numerous play quartos, including some non-Shakespearean ones, to Shakespeare, either by name or initials, and we may assume that they deemed Shakespeare's name and supposed authorship, true or false, commercially attractive.

For the next ten years or so, various records show Shakespeare's dual career as playwright and man of the theater in London, and as an important local figure in Stratford. In 1608-9 his acting company – designated the "King's Men" soon after King James had succeeded Queen Elizabeth in 1603 – rented, refurbished, and opened a small interior playing space, the Blackfriars theater, in London, and Shakespeare was once again listed as a substantial sharer in the group of proprietors of the playhouse. By May 11, 1612, however, he describes himself as a Stratford resident in a London lawsuit – an indication that he had withdrawn from day-to-day professional activity and returned to the town where he had always had his main financial interests. When Shakespeare bought a substantial residential building in London, the Blackfriars Gatehouse, close to the theater of the same name, on March 10, 1613, he is recorded as William Shakespeare "of Stratford upon Avon in the county of Warwick, gentleman," and he named several London residents as the building's trustees. Still, he continued to participate in theatrical activity: when the new Earl of Rutland needed an allegorical design to bear as a shield, or *impresa,* at the celebration of King James's Accession Day, March 24, 1613, the earl's accountant recorded a payment of 44 shillings to Shakespeare for the device with its motto.

For the last few years of his life, Shakespeare evidently

concentrated his activities in the town of his birth. Most of the final records concern business transactions in Stratford, ending with the notation of his death on April 23, 1616, and burial in Holy Trinity Church, Stratford-upon-Avon.

## THE QUESTION OF AUTHORSHIP

The history of ascribing Shakespeare's plays (the poems do not come up so often) to someone else began, as it continues, peculiarly. The earliest published claim that someone else wrote Shakespeare's plays appeared in an 1856 article by Delia Bacon in the American journal *Putnam's Monthly* – although an Englishman, Thomas Wilmot, had shared his doubts in private (even secretive) conversations with friends near the end of the eighteenth century. Bacon's was a sad personal history that ended in madness and poverty, but the year after her article, she published, with great difficulty and the bemused assistance of Nathaniel Hawthorne (then United States Consul in Liverpool, England), her *Philosophy of the Plays of Shakspere Unfolded.* This huge, ornately written, confusing farrago is almost unreadable; sometimes its intents, to say nothing of its arguments, disappear entirely beneath near-raving, ecstatic writing. Tumbled in with much supposed "philosophy" appear the claims that Francis Bacon (from whom Delia Bacon eventually claimed descent), Walter Ralegh, and several other contemporaries of Shakespeare's had written the plays. The book had little impact except as a ridiculed curiosity.

Once proposed, however, the issue gained momentum among people whose conviction was the greater in proportion to their ignorance of sixteenth- and seventeenth-century English literature, history, and society. Another American amateur, Catherine P. Ashmead Windle, made the next influential contribution to the cause when she published *Report to the British Museum* (1882), wherein she promised to open "the Cipher of Francis Bacon," though what she mostly offers, in the words of S. Schoenbaum, is "demented allegorizing." An entire new cottage industry grew from Windle's suggestion that the texts contain hidden, cryptographically discoverable ciphers – "clues" – to their authorship; and today there are not only books devoted to the putative ciphers, but also pamphlets, journals, and newsletters.

Although Baconians have led the pack of those seeking a substitute Shakespeare, in *"Shakespeare" Identified* (1920), J. Thomas Looney became the first published "Oxfordian" when he proposed Edward de Vere, seventeenth earl of Oxford, as the secret author of Shakespeare's plays. Also for Oxford and his "authorship" there are today dedicated societies, articles, journals, and books. Less popular candidates – Queen Elizabeth and Christopher Marlowe among them – have had adherents, but the movement seems to have divided into two main contending factions, Baconian and Oxfordian. (For further details on all the candidates for "Shakespeare," see S. Schoenbaum, *Shakespeare's Lives,* 2nd ed., 1991.)

The Baconians, the Oxfordians, and supporters of other candidates have one trait in common – they are snobs. Every pro-Bacon or pro-Oxford tract sooner or later claims that the historical William Shakespeare of Stratford-upon-Avon could not have written the plays because he could not have had the training, the university education, the experience, and indeed the imagination or background their author supposedly possessed. Only a learned genius like Bacon or an aristocrat like Oxford could have written such fine plays. (As it happens, lucky male children of the middle class had access to better education than most aristocrats in Elizabethan England – and Oxford was not particularly well educated.) Shakespeare received in the Stratford grammar school a formal education that would daunt many college graduates today; and popular rival playwrights such as the very learned Ben Jonson and George Chapman, both of whom also lacked university training, achieved great artistic success, without being taken as Bacon or Oxford.

Besides snobbery, one other quality characterizes the authorship controversy: lack of evidence. A great deal of testimony from Shakespeare's time shows that Shakespeare wrote Shakespeare's plays and that his contemporaries recognized them as distinctive and distinctly superior. (Some of that contemporary evidence is collected in E. K. Chambers, *William Shakespeare: A Study of Facts and Problems,* 2 vols., 1930.) Since that testimony comes from Shakespeare's enemies and theatrical competitors as well as from his co-workers and from the Elizabethan equivalent of literary journalists, it seems unlikely that, if any of these sources had known he was a fraud, they would have failed to record that fact.

## Books About Shakespeare's Theater

Useful scholarly studies of theatrical life in Shakespeare's day include: G. E. Bentley, *The Jacobean and Caroline Stage,* 7 vols. (1941–68), and the same author's *The Professions of Dramatist and Player in Shakespeare's Time, 1590–1642* (1986); E. K. Chambers, *The Elizabethan Stage,* 4 vols. (1923); R. A. Foakes, *Illustrations of the English Stage, 1580–1642* (1985); Andrew Gurr, *The Shakespearean Stage,* 3rd ed. (1992), and the same author's *Play-going in Shakespeare's London,* 2nd ed. (1996); Edwin Nungezer, *A Dictionary of Actors* (1929); Carol Chillington Rutter, ed., *Documents of the Rose Playhouse* (1984).

## Books About Shakespeare's Life

The following books provide scholarly, documented accounts of Shakespeare's life: G. E. Bentley, *Shakespeare: A Biographical Handbook* (1961); E. K. Chambers, *William Shakespeare: A Study of Facts and Problems,* 2 vols. (1930); S. Schoenbaum, *William Shakespeare: A Compact*

*Documentary Life* (1977); and *Shakespeare's Lives,* 2nd ed. (1991), by the same author. Many scholarly editions of Shakespeare's complete works print brief compilations of essential dates and events. References to Shakespeare's works up to 1700 are collected in C. M. Ingleby et al., *The Shakespeare Allusion-Book,* rev. ed., 2 vols. (1932).

# The Texts of Shakespeare

As FAR AS WE KNOW, only one manuscript conceivably in Shakespeare's own hand may (and even this is much disputed) exist: a few pages of a play called *Sir Thomas More*, which apparently was never performed. What we do have, as later readers, performers, scholars, students, are printed texts. The earliest of these survive in two forms: quartos and folios. Quartos (from the Latin for "four") are small books, printed on sheets of paper that were then folded in fours, to make eight double-sided pages. When these were bound together, the result was a squarish, eminently portable volume that sold for the relatively small sum of sixpence (translating in modern terms to about $5.00). In folios, on the other hand, the sheets are folded only once, in half, producing large, impressive volumes taller than they are wide. This was the format for important works of philosophy, science, theology, and literature (the major precedent for a folio Shakespeare was Ben Jonson's *Works*, 1616). The decision to print the works of a popular playwright in folio is an indication of how far up on the social scale the theatrical profession had come during Shakespeare's lifetime. The Shakespeare folio was an expensive book, selling for between fifteen and eighteen shillings, depending on the binding (in modern terms, from about $150 to $180). Twenty Shakespeare plays of the thirty-seven that survive first appeared in quarto, seventeen of which appeared during Shakespeare's lifetime; the rest of the plays are found only in folio.

The First Folio was published in 1623, seven years after Shakespeare's death, and was authorized by his fellow actors, the co-owners of the King's Men. This publication

was certainly a mark of the company's enormous respect
for Shakespeare; but it was also a way of turning the old
plays, most of which were no longer current in the playhouse, into ready money (the folio includes only Shakespeare's plays, not his sonnets or other nondramatic verse).
Whatever the motives behind the publication of the folio,
the texts it preserves constitute the basis for almost all later
editions of the playwright's works. The texts, however, differ from those of the earlier quartos, sometimes in minor
respects but often significantly – most strikingly in the
two texts of *King Lear*, but also in important ways in
*Hamlet, Othello,* and *Troilus and Cressida.* (The variants
are recorded in the textual notes to each play in the new
Pelican series.) The differences in these texts represent, in
a sense, the essence of theater: the texts of plays were initially not intended for publication. They were scripts, designed for the actors to perform – the principal life of the
play at this period was in performance. And it follows that
in Shakespeare's theater the playwright typically had no
say either in how his play was performed or in the disposition of his text – he was an employee of the company. The
authoritative figures in the theatrical enterprise were the
shareholders in the company, who were for the most part
the major actors. They decided what plays were to be
done; they hired the playwright and often gave him an
outline of the play they wanted him to write. Often, too,
the play was a collaboration: the company would retain a
group of writers, and parcel out the scenes among them.
The resulting script was then the property of the company, and the actors would revise it as they saw fit during
the course of putting it on stage. The resulting text belonged to the company. The playwright had no rights in it
once he had been paid. (This system survives largely intact
in the movie industry, and most of the playwrights of
Shakespeare's time were as anonymous as most screenwrit-
ers are today.) The script could also, of course, continue to

change as the tastes of audiences and the requirements of the actors changed. Many – perhaps most – plays were revised when they were reintroduced after any substantial absence from the repertory, or when they were performed by a company different from the one that originally commissioned the play.

Shakespeare was an exceptional figure in this world because he was not only a shareholder and actor in his company, but also its leading playwright – he was literally his own boss. He had, moreover, little interest in the publication of his plays, and even those that appeared during his lifetime with the authorization of the company show no signs of any editorial concern on the part of the author. Theater was, for Shakespeare, a fluid and supremely responsive medium – the very opposite of the great classic canonical text that has embodied his works since 1623.

The very fluidity of the original texts, however, has meant that Shakespeare has always had to be edited. Here is an example of how problematic the editorial project inevitably is, a passage from the most famous speech in *Romeo and Juliet,* Juliet's balcony soliloquy beginning "O Romeo, Romeo, wherefore art thou Romeo?" Since the eighteenth century, the standard modern text has read,

> What's Montague? It is nor hand, nor foot,
> Nor arm, nor face, nor any other part
> Belonging to a man. O be some other name!
> What's in a name? That which we call a rose
> By any other name would smell as sweet.
>
> (II.2.40-44)

Editors have three early texts of this play to work from, two quarto texts and the folio. Here is how the First Quarto (1597) reads:

> Whats *Mountague*? It is nor band nor foote,
> Nor arme, nor face, nor any other part.
> Whats in a name? That which we call a Rose,
> By any other name would smell as sweet:

Here is the Second Quarto (1599):

> Whats *Mountague*? it is nor hand nor foote,
> Nor arme nor face, ô be some other name
> Belonging to a man.
> Whats in a name that which we call a rose,
> By any other word would smell as sweete,

And here is the First Folio (1623):

> What's *Mountague*? it is nor hand nor foote,
> Nor arme, nor face, O be some other name
> Belonging to a man.
> What? in a names that which we call a Rose,
> By any other word would smell as sweete,

There is in fact no early text that reads as our modern text does – and this is the most famous speech in the play. Instead, we have three quite different texts, all of which are clearly some version of the same speech, but none of which seems to us a final or satisfactory version. The transcendently beautiful passage in modern editions is an editorial invention: editors have succeeded in conflating and revising the three versions into something we recognize as great poetry. Is this what Shakespeare "really" wrote? Who can say? What we can say is that Shakespeare always had performance, not a book, in mind.

## Books About the Shakespeare Texts

The standard study of the printing history of the First Folio is W. W. Greg, *The Shakespeare First Folio* (1955). J. K. Walton, *The Quarto Copy for the First Folio of Shakespeare*

(1971), is a useful survey of the relation of the quartos to the folio. The second edition of Charlton Hinman's *Norton Facsimile* of the First Folio (1996), with a new introduction by Peter Blayney, is indispensable. Stanley Wells, Gary Taylor, John Jowett, and William Montgomery, *William Shakespeare: A Textual Companion,* keyed to the Oxford text, gives a comprehensive survey of the editorial situation for all the plays and poems.

THE GENERAL EDITORS

# Introduction

ALTHOUGH *The Life of King Henry the Eighth* is a remarkable and highly rewarding play, it is underappreciated at present, having been increasingly overshadowed in the twentieth century by Shakespeare's earlier histories, from *Richard II* through *Henry V.* Before the twentieth century, in fact, the play was a popular one, and was regularly performed with notable success. Sir William Davenant revived it after the Restoration in 1660, and made it one of the great spectacle plays of the age – the diarist Samuel Pepys liked it enough to see it twice. Colley Cibber mounted a sumptuous production in 1727 in honor of the coronation of George II, and added a great deal of pageantry, including a coronation scene. Ironically, it was, of course, Anne Bullen, historically doomed to execution, who was crowned. This set piece succeeded so well that it was added to other plays as a pantomime, and in that one season the coronation from *Henry VIII* was performed seventy-five times. David Garrick kept it in the repertory, as did John Philip Kemble; in the nineteenth century there were major productions by William Macready, Charles Kean, and Sir Henry Irving. The great, virtuoso roles (even today practically foolproof in the theater) were those of Wolsey and Queen Katherine, played in Irving's production, in 1892, by Irving himself and Ellen Terry. Sir Herbert Beerbohm Tree's production, in 1910, was considered a theatrical revelation – as one critic put it, "the most gorgeous thing ever attempted in this country in that line of staging."* With its elaborately scripted

---

* G.C.D. O'Dell, *Shakespeare from Betterton to Irving* (New York, 1920), II, p. 464.

scenes of pageantry, *Henry VIII* peculiarly lent itself to opulent staging.

Both a radically changed view of English history and a twentieth-century reaction against the lavish, pictorial stagings of the Victorian era no doubt help to account for the play's relative neglect in modern times. Another important reason for the play's eclipse, however, has surely been the belief, originating in the late nineteenth century, that the play was written only in part by Shakespeare. There is no external evidence to support this view, yet perceived anomalies of style, diction, and poetic quality in the play prompted speculation that *Henry VIII* might have been coauthored by Shakespeare and one or more contemporary playwrights.

*The Two Noble Kinsmen,* for example, is ascribed on its title page to Shakespeare and John Fletcher, and Fletcher is also named in the Stationers' Register as Shakespeare's collaborator in a now lost play called *Cardenio.* Since Fletcher was Shakespeare's successor as principal dramatist for the King's Men, he remains the favored candidate for coauthorship of *Henry VIII.* Most critics and editors have found the coauthorship thesis convincing, although they have differed quite widely in their views about the respective contributions of Shakespeare, Fletcher, and possible others. Fletcher has been credited with the title *All Is True,* under which the play appears to have been first performed in 1613, yet the title under which the play was published, *The Famous History of the Life of King Henry the Eight[h],* has generally been credited to Shakespeare or the editors of the 1623 folio edition of his plays. (The folio text is the sole printed source for *Henry VIII.*)

Although the question of the play's authorship is an important and legitimate one, discussion of it has tended to preempt other critical concerns and exclude *Henry VIII* from consideration as an authentic Shakespearean play. The loss is ours. There is no escaping the fact that the play was included as Shakespeare's in the 1623 folio, edited by his fellow actors, who were in the best position to know. That ascription was never questioned, as I have said, before the late nineteenth century. In principle, *Henry VIII* must therefore count as a play by Shakespeare until decisively proven otherwise. To date, neither the intuitions of critics nor statistical analyses of the play's language and diction have disqualified it from full consideration within the Shakespearean canon. Indeed, the more systematically critics have tried to map the play's deviations from supposed Shakespearean norms, the more questionable those norms have come to seem, and the less capable of determining what is or is not definitively Shakespearean.

Even if coauthorship were proven, however, the fact wouldn't necessarily detract from the interest of the play or diminish Shakespeare's investment in it. Much recent criticism has shown that collaboration in the production of sixteenth- and seventeenth-century texts, especially play texts, was more normal than anomalous. The fact that a play carried a particular author's name never precluded revisions and additions by several "hands," and the actors, editors, and scribes who prepared the plays for the press contributed to the printed texts. The survival of so many plays by Shakespeare and his contemporaries in markedly different versions implies a lack of exclusive authorial control over the text (or its revisions) at any point in its publication history. Moreover, plays were the property of the acting companies, not of their named authors, and therefore not under the authors' control. Modern attachment to the imagined fact and value of sole, controlling authorship – the form of authorship still too often regarded as the very basis of literary merit or authenticity – is foreign to the world in which Shakespeare's plays were produced. There can be little doubt, however, that anachronistic devotion to the ideal of Shakespeare's sole authorship has hurt the fortunes of the supposedly collaborative *Henry VIII* in modern times.

Hardly less to be regretted, the coauthorship theory regarding *Henry VIII* has failed to live up to its own potential for generating interest in the play. Recent criticism has increasingly paid attention to Shakespeare's tendency, late in his playwriting career, to embrace coauthorship actively as an authorial mode. *Pericles, The Two Noble Kinsmen,* and the lost *Cardenio* were evidently coauthored by Shakespeare. To regard this coauthorship simply as evidence of Shakespeare's decline, semiretirement, or withdrawal from the full rigors of composition begs the question. As other critics have pointed out, this prejudicial view has been supported by the persistent myth that *The Tempest* (1611) was Shakespeare's last play, in which, as solo dramatist, he took his formal leave of the stage. Although that myth has negative consequences in general, it is particularly damaging to *Henry VIII*. That play was not only written after *The Tempest,* but has no less a claim to count as Shakespeare's last word.

Rather than diminishing the interest of *Henry VIII,* consideration of its possible coauthorship might in fact add to its interest; it could also expand our understanding of the last phase of Shakespeare's playwriting career. The avowed coauthorship of Francis Beaumont and John Fletcher, whose plays were very popular, gave a certain trendiness to coauthorship around the time *Henry VIII* was written. As the work of Jeffrey Masten among others has suggested, the avowed coauthorship of Beaumont and Fletcher, roughly coinciding with that of Shakespeare and Fletcher, provides a model for authorial bonding, interaction, and transference at odds with that of sole authorship. It is a model importantly at odds, what is more, with that of authorship as a phenomenon of male competition and compulsive self-assertion only. The point isn't that Shakespeare had no investment in his own authorship and no part in competitive authorial self-fashioning – his work gives ample evidence of both – but that collaboration was a phenomenon of the time that would clearly be embraced as an active option, even by Shakespeare.

Given that recent critiques of the sole-authorship fetish have now opened the way to renewed appreciation of *Henry VIII,* then, what features internal to the play might additionally explain its current neglect? Perhaps the most likely ones from the point of view of both staging and readership are, first, the play's reliance on reported rather than dramatically presented action; second, the play's relatively "transparent" rather than metaphorically dense language; third, the absence of larger-than-life entertainers like the Falstaff of *Henry IV,* Parts 1 and 2; and, last, a historical frame more restricted than the huge panoramic one of the history plays from *Richard II* through *Henry V* (or, indeed, from *Henry VI,* Parts 1, 2, and 3, through *Richard III*). The narrowing of the frame in *Henry VIII* coincides with a reduction in the sheer variety and exuberance of the earlier histories, and perhaps with a lowering of the dramatic intensity. Yet to regard *Henry VIII* as "lacking" on these counts is to refuse its specific dramaturgical challenges and achievements, including its possible critique of the earlier history plays. A Shakespeare who changes rather than repeats himself (or tries to repeat his earlier successes) is an interesting figure who calls for recognition in *Henry VIII.*

What, then, characterizes *Henry VIII* as the last of Shakespeare's English history plays, positioned as such in the folio immediately before the tragedies? What history does it relate, and how does it do so? The play is quite closely based on historical chronicles, mainly those of Raphael Holinshed (1587) and Edward Hall (1548). John Foxe's *Book of Martyrs* is a source for Act V. George Cavendish's *Negotiations of Cardinal Wolsey,* widely circulated in manuscript, though not published until 1641, may have been at least an indirect source. The play begins shortly after a celebrated peacemaking encounter in 1520 between Henry VIII and Francis I, King of France, in Picardy. This encounter took place on what came to be known as the Field of the Cloth of Gold, and was marked by elaborate displays and ceremonials, with each king seeking to outshine the other in opulent pageantry. Characteristically, this encounter is reported rather than witnessed in *Henry VIII,* and its effects prove short-lived. Both the emulous rivalry of the kings and traditional English xenophobia soon reassert themselves; the latter does so comically insofar as it turns out to be based on the fear that stylish French men are more sexually appealing to women than their English counterparts. Peace with France threatens to make Englishmen permanent losers in the arena of heterosexual competition.

All of this can hardly fail to recall both Shakespeare's *Henry V* and the long-standing national rivalry between the French and the English. Yet in *Henry VIII* that national rivalry, with its prospect of ever-renewed conflict, proves inconsequential. English domestic politics – the literally domestic politics of royal divorce and remarriage – soon take precedence. Neither historically nor in the play is Henry VIII destined to be another conquering English military leader on the model of Henry V. Nor will national destiny and identity remain closely tied to rivalry with France. *Henry VIII* thus actively revises a popular as well as apparently compelling nationalistic scenario of the earlier history plays.

Some readers of *Henry VIII* have, indeed, found it disappointing that the only pitched battle (a reported one at that) is fought with cudgels between porters and unruly, youthful revelers at the christening ceremonies for Elizabeth I at the end of the play, those revelers apparently belonging to something like modern youth gangs. Anticlimactic farce rather than heroic victory thus characterizes "warfare" in *Henry VIII;* perhaps the play is making a point about the exaggerated importance given to military action in both drama and history. Indeed, the marked distancing of action in *Henry VIII,* a feature that may make the play seem more neoclassically old-fashioned than Shakespeare's earlier history plays, is systematic.

That not only allows pageant and spectacle, scripted with unusual elaborateness in this play, to come to the fore, but implies that political spectacle, performance, and stage management are themselves the matter of history. Henry clearly gains command as king when he emerges from under the sway of Wolsey's eloquence and stage management, and begins to control both the language and staging of power himself. His mastery of Wolsey is manifested by the confidence with which he begins to deploy irony against him, after Wolsey has fatally betrayed his own double-dealing. Indeed, it is almost as if the overreaching Wolsey acts under a compulsion to undo himself, while Henry, like Prospero in *The Tempest* anticipating the propitious moment that delivers his enemies into his hands, awaits the pretext that will allow him to take control.

The narrative of *Henry VIII* is focused on some of the key personalities and events of Henry VIII's reign. Or, as Sir Henry Wotton said in a letter written in 1613, it "represent[s] some principal pieces of the reign of Henry 8." These include Henry himself as title character; the ambitious, conniving Cardinal Wolsey, Henry's Lord Chancellor when the play begins; Katherine of Aragon, the Spanish-born wife Henry divorces in order to marry Anne Bullen; Anne Bullen herself; the Duke of Buckingham, condemned to death for treason early in the play (Wolsey being widely held responsible for his fall); Stephen Gardiner, Bishop of Winchester and a defender of the Catholic faith already threatened by Protestant reform in England; and Thomas Cranmer, who becomes the Archbishop of Canterbury in the course of the play. The cast includes numerous secondary or minor characters, but ones of some significance even when they are only spectators of the pageants being staged by the great.

These are the main events of the play: Buckingham's execution; Henry's falling in love with Anne Bullen; the process through which Henry's marriage to Katherine gets annulled on the technical grounds that she had been lawfully wedded, in a consummated marriage, to his deceased elder brother Arthur (and thus that her subsequent marriage to Henry was incestuous under canon law); the fall of Wolsey and his replacement as Lord Chancellor by Sir Thomas More; the rise of Cranmer, already on his way to becoming the first English Protestant Archbishop of Canterbury; the birth of Anne's daughter Elizabeth, destined to rule as Queen of England; and, finally, the public festivities attending Elizabeth's christening, during which the "truth-telling" Cranmer prophesies her glorious reign to come.

As this summary indicates, the play very selectively covers some significant moments and personalities during the reign of Henry VIII. It omits a great deal from this reign, however, by ending with the birth of Elizabeth. Shakespeare's contemporaries would have known of the subsequent English break with the Catholic church, of Anne Bullen's execution on charges of treason and infidelity, of Thomas More's execution and replacement as Lord Chancellor by Thomas Cromwell, of Henry's four subsequent marriages, and of his death. Although the play is titled the "life" of Henry VIII, it stops far short of the end; in fact, it stops at the moment when Henry feels creatively reborn through the birth of his child – who, in one of the strangest moments of the play, is initially reported to him as a son – and thus like the paternal founder of a great nation rather than merely the inheritor of a kingdom. Unlike Katherine's daughter Mary, Elizabeth will apparently count as a son, and more. The rest lies beyond the frame of the play. Perhaps we are to understand that this residue has been rendered inconsequential, less by the birth of the miraculous Elizabeth, queen of the future, than by the presence on the throne, in 1613, of her male successor, James I.

Shakespeare's choosing to end the narrative at that point says much about his purposes in the play. The choice helps to explain, without explaining away, his omissions, chronological alterations, and contentious interpretations of the historical record even before the birth of Elizabeth in the play. (Many of these would have been as glaringly obvious to Shakespeare's contemporaries as they are to modern scholars.) In *Henry VIII,* as in all his history plays, Shakespeare's interest in English history is neither passive nor impartial. On the contrary, it is a strongly participatory, shaping interest in what we might now call the English national narrative: that is to say, the continuing story – or interwoven stories – of English national formation, mutating identity, and destiny. That interest was not Shakespeare's alone – indeed, for his plays to make sense to others, it could hardly have been his alone – but one capable of being shared with, and modified by, a host of collaborators, both on the stage and off. Concluding *Henry VIII* with the birth of Elizabeth orients the play toward the distant future rather than the concluding events of Henry's reign. The national destiny prophesied in the play, whether through Cranmer's visionary concluding speech or by implication elsewhere in the play, includes the foundation of a global empire: the play includes allusions to the wealth of the Indies and to English expansion into the New World through the Virginia colony. (Even racial mythology is already in the air as the play alludes to the New World Indian with his "great tool," V.3.32.)

Although Shakespeare was certainly not unaware of the provincialism and folly of aggressive English patriotism (a consciousness built into *Cymbeline,* for example), the production of large national narratives was one of the compelling projects of European political cultures as well as individual writers in Shakespeare's time. In that era of rapid national formation and assertion, there was no escaping the fact that the nation had become a principal unit of political and imaginative consciousness as well as of historical development. Shakespeare's part in scripting the English, Protestant, national narrative is clearly a major one, and *Henry VIII* contributes both distinctively and crucially to that enterprise.

In the context of that enterprise, the increasingly belea-guered Catholic power represented by Cardinal Wolsey in *Henry VIII* harks back to an earlier political epoch, one in which Western Europe could conceive of itself as the Holy Roman Empire, a unitary political entity under the spiritual command of Rome. We hear during the play that Wolsey had hoped to become Bishop of Toledo in Spain; he has no national attachment, and can hope to pursue his ambitions anywhere in Europe. The fall of Wolsey in *Henry VIII* thus represents the passing of an an-cient political era, "catholic" in both senses of the term. In the course of the play, the independence of the English kingdom and the subordination of religious to national, political authority become increasingly entrenched; by the same token, Henry is increasingly "liberated" from Wolsey's arrogant domination and attempted manipula-tion. Although the strong-minded Katherine is almost ha-giographically presented in the play as a model spouse and Christian woman, she nevertheless remains, even in her own mind, a Spanish "stranger." When Wolsey sees the divorce coming, he plans to marry Henry off to the sister of the French king (historically, Marguerite of Navarre, author of the *Heptaméron*), but before he can act, Henry has already married Anne on his own initia-tive. She, in contrast to the foreigners, is definitively an English beauty with childbearing potential. Indeed, un-like Katherine, who offers the king political advice, Anne is little more than a woman whose potentially disruptive sexuality will be conscripted for dynastic purposes. Mar-riage legitimizes formerly illicit relations between Henry and Anne, just as christening sanctifies the offspring of that union. Significantly, the threat of both political and sexual "disorder," including miscegenation, reappears at the moment of the christening through the comically indignant perceptions of the porter:

> What should you do but knock 'em down by th'
> dozens? Is this Moorfields to muster in? Or have we
> some strange Indian with the great tool come to
> court, the women so besiege us? Bless me, what a
> fry of fornication is at door! On my Christian con-
> science this one christening will beget a thousand;
> here will be father, godfather, and all together.
>
> (V.3.30-36)

The porter's vision of social upheaval conflates women's supposedly inordinate sexual appetites with plebeian riot and lust for colonial natives. Not only does the distinction between natural and spiritual paternity (father/god-father) collapse, but reproduction runs out of control in a prolific begetting of anonymous thousands. In marked contrast, the birth and christening of Elizabeth represent controlled, economical, purposeful reproduction in the service of political order and national propagation. The threat of disorder surfaces only to be dispelled. What will henceforth be reproduced in England is pure Englishness, a fact at least as consequential as political rivalry with other European nations.

Spectators in the play report that Anne has been exposed to public view during the coronation ceremonies. We hear that her beauty elicited thrilled public comment and approval for the remarriage. This display may strike us as a distasteful form of publicity, she being put onstage as a politically exploitable object of desire and perhaps as Henry's new trophy wife. Yet she is also being displayed as the mother of Elizabeth, thus underlining the crucial importance of reproduction and succession to the shaping of a national destiny. Moreover, the birth of Elizabeth, even though she is not the wished-for son, enables Henry to feel empowered both as a man and a king, especially after

Cranmer has framed the event to Henry's liking. Not even Elizabeth's famed virginity, also prophesied by Cranmer, will interrupt this royal succession, since Cranmer's prophecy includes the "miracle" by which James I, not a biological heir, will succeed Elizabeth:

> as when
> The bird of wonder dies, the maiden phoenix,
> Her ashes new create another heir
> As great in admiration as herself,
> So shall she leave her blessedness to one
> (When heaven shall call her from this cloud
>    of darkness)
> Who from the sacred ashes of her honor
> Shall starlike rise, as great in fame as she was,
> And so stand fixed.
>
> (V.4.39-47)

Critics have often noted that *Henry VIII* shares many traits with Shakespeare's late "romances" (*Pericles, Cymbeline, A Winter's Tale*). The motifs of miraculous birth or recovery of a daughter, of adult rebirth of the king, of verified prophecy, and of a providential outcome to the seemingly incalculable vicissitudes and manifold corruptions of history are among the "romance" elements of *Henry VIII*. In this play, however, such romance motifs remain at the service of the national narrative. They not only contribute to the narrative but draw attention to its necessarily imaginative, fictionalized, and inspirational character – or, to put it more negatively, its bondage to fantasy and wish fulfillment rather than historical veracity. The play's alternative title, *All Is True,* can thus be read as mordantly ironic: "all is false" would make equal sense, a fact that wouldn't necessarily have escaped some of Shakespeare's contemporaries. Yet that wholly ironic reading is historically implausible, and in any case the title *All Is True* preempts distinctions between truth and falsity, history and fiction, that might be applied to the play. Undoing such distinctions as a source, not of ethical choice but of sterile contention and anxiety, forms a large part of Shakespeare's late "romance" agenda. So does the inculcation of belief that truth does or will prevail everywhere. The appearance of falsity is thus either immaterial or ultimately another manifestation of truth: such is the leap of faith for which romance calls upon us.

The national destiny Cranmer prophesies at Elizabeth's christening links the historical past to the present in which the play was being written and performed. It is a prophecy that anticipates the full course of Elizabeth's reign and the succession of James I; it has therefore already been "verified" in large measure by the time of the play's performance in 1613. Shakespearean hindsight, in other words, informs the prophecy spoken by Cranmer in *Henry VIII*.

Critics seeking to explain why *Henry VIII* was particularly timely in 1613 have suggested that the play was intended to "recall" James I to the historic destiny of which he was the principal bearer, and to re-instill in him an elevated vision of his kingship, compromised as it had become by political corruption, vacillation, and mismanagement. It has convincingly been argued, in any event, that *Henry VIII* alludes directly to the marriage of James I's daughter Elizabeth to Prince Frederick, Elector Palatine and leader of German Protestants, on February 14, 1613. Shakespeare and others may well have seen that event as a timely reassertion of national, Protestant values and English leadership – James was often suspected of being soft on Catholicism – in which, at the same time, the glories of the first Elizabeth were being recalled. Jacobean nostalgia for Elizabeth I has been well documented by critics; a 1613 play ending with the *birth* of Elizabeth certainly attests to the continuing hold on the imagination of the late queen, exceeding that of her "famous" father.

The play's representation of Henry VIII's reign, then,

including its emphases and omissions, appears largely determined by the exigencies of the national narrative. That narrative is, in turn, being constructed in ways that differ significantly from those of the earlier history plays. What *Henry VIII* apparently offered contemporary English audiences was a revision and updating of the national narrative, emphasizing the "miracle" of royal succession, into which they could incorporate themselves. That some, perhaps many, chose to do so seems likely (that is one possible explanation for the play's apparently good reception in the theater), but the play certainly leaves room for reservations and even dissenting views. Strong polarization and communal fragmentation are thereby avoided. As previously mentioned, the play's "losers" – Buckingham, Wolsey, and, above all, Katherine – have prevailed in the play's stage history as its most engaging characters in performance; their great, concluding set pieces have often been excerpted from the play for theatrical recital. None of these characters is demonized as an antagonist of the national destiny. Hatred for Wolsey in the play seems generally based on the envious resentment and class disdain of the aristocracy, while not even Henry has a word to say against Katherine, even though he plans to divorce her. All these characters leave the stage with dignity, their "fall" from greatness being staged with some of the stylized, ceremonious formality and pathos of medieval tragedy. (As is the case with the play's reporting of action, an "old-fashioned" dramaturgy is being linked here to a contemporary purpose – namely, that of allowing those overtaken by history to depart at peace, without threatening to return and haunt the living.) The pageant staged at the death of Katherine, which she sees as a heavenly vision, belongs to a different genre from the pageants so lavishly orchestrated in the service of power by Wolsey and the king: she inhabits a different order from the one they inhabit. The frame of this play, like those of the Shakespearean romances, can evidently accommodate incommensurable realities. Perhaps that is another implication of the title *All Is True*.

To conclude, then, *Henry VIII* is a play that eminently deserves full recognition within the Shakespearean canon. Discussion either of the history plays or of Shakespeare's national vision that slights *Henry VIII* is unquestionably deficient. Moreover, we may hope that the merits of the play will increasingly vie for interest with the best-known historical fact about it: during one of its performances in 1613, the Globe theater burned down, its thatched roof having caught fire after a discharge of cannons (the cannons probably having been those fired to announce the arrival of the king and his party at Wolsey's banquet in Act I, scene 4). That event, colorfully reported in the 1613 letter by Sir Henry Wotton already cited, has done more than anything else to etch the play in modern consciousness, but repetition of the story sometimes conveys the implication that only an unusual accident lends interest to *Henry VIII*. The play deserves far better than that.

JONATHAN CREWE
*Dartmouth College*

# Note on the Text

*H*ENRY VIII WAS first printed in the 1623 folio volume of Shakespeare's plays. It appears as the last of the English history plays, immediately before the tragedies. The text is carefully printed, and relatively free of apparent errors and anomalies. Unlike some previous modern editions, this one fully adheres to the folio act and scene divisions. The spelling of names has been regularized, and inconsistencies in the speech prefixes have been resolved. I have incorporated a substantial number of glosses from the earlier Pelican text edited by F. David Hoeniger. Substantive departures from the folio are listed below, with the adopted reading in italics followed by the folio reading in roman.

I.1 42–47 *All . . . together* (assigned to Buckingham in F)    63 *web, a* Web.
O    69–70 *that? / . . . hell the* that, / . . . Hell? The    79–80 *council
out, / . . . in he* Councell, out / . . . in, he    96 *Bordeaux* Burdeux    120
*venom-mouthed* venom'd-mouth'd    123 *chafed* chaff'd    200 *Hereford*
Hertford    219 *Perk* Pecke; *chancellor* Councellour
I.2 67 *business* basenesse    156 *feared* feare    164 *confession's* Commissions
180 *To* For this to    190 *Bulmer* Blumer    191 *time. Being* time, being
I.3 59 *wherewithal. In him* wherewithall in him;
II.1 20 *Perk* Pecke    86 *mark* make
II.3 14 *quarrel, fortune, do* quarrel. Fortune, do    32 *cheveril* Chiverell    59
*note's* notes    61 *of you, and* of you, and    of you;
II.4 131 *Exeunt* Exit    172 *A* And    197 *throe* throw    217 *summons. Un-
solicited* Summons unsolicited
III.1 23 s.d. *Campeius* Campian    61 *your* our    83 *profit. Can* profit can
124 *accursed* a curse
III.2 142 *glad* gald    233 *commission, lords?* Commission? Lords,    343
*Chattels* Castels
IV.1 20 SECOND GENTLEMAN    34 *Kimbolton* Kymmalton    36 s.d., item 4
*Choristers* Quirristers    54–56 SECOND GENTLEMAN *Their . . . / FIRST
GENTLEMAN And . . . SECOND GENTLEMAN No . . . / FIRST GENTLEMAN
God . . . 2* Their . . . / And . . . 2 No . . . / 1 God . . .    78 *press* prease
101 *Stokely* Stokesly

IV.2 7 *think* thank   82 **s.d.** *reverent* reverend
V.1 37 *time* Lime   55 *Exeunt* Exit   139 *precipice* Precepit
V.2 8 *piece* Peere   120, 122 *CHANCELLOR* Cham.   207 *brother love*
Brother; loue
V.3 81 *press* praesse
V.4 37 *ways* way

# The Life of King Henry
## the Eighth

# [Names of the Actors

KING HENRY THE EIGHTH
CARDINAL WOLSEY
CARDINAL CAMPEIUS
CAPUCHIUS, *ambassador from the Emperor Charles V*
CRANMER, *Archbishop of Canterbury*
DUKE OF NORFOLK
DUKE OF BUCKINGHAM
DUKE OF SUFFOLK
EARL OF SURREY
LORD CHAMBERLAIN
LORD CHANCELLOR
GARDINER, *King Henry's secretary, afterward Bishop of Winchester*
BISHOP OF LINCOLN
LORD ABERGAVENNY
LORD SANDYS *(Sir Walter Sandys)*
SIR HENRY GUILFORD
SIR THOMAS LOVELL
SIR ANTHONY DENNY
SIR NICHOLAS VAUX
BRANDON*
CROMWELL, *servant to Wolsey*
GRIFFITH, *gentleman usher to Queen Katherine*
THREE GENTLEMEN
DOCTOR BUTTS, *physician to the King*
GARTER KING-OF-ARMS

---

* *Brandon* (perhaps identical with the Duke of Suffolk above, whose name was Charles Brandon)

SURVEYOR TO THE DUKE OF BUCKINGHAM
DOORKEEPER OF THE COUNCIL CHAMBER
SERGEANT AT ARMS
PORTER, AND HIS MAN
PAGE TO GARDINER
SECRETARIES TO WOLSEY
A CRIER
QUEEN KATHERINE, *wife to King Henry, afterward divorced*
ANNE BULLEN, *her Maid of Honor, afterward Queen*
OLD LADY, *friend to Anne Bullen*
PATIENCE, *woman to Queen Katherine*
SPIRITS
LORDS, LADIES, BISHOPS, JUDGES, GENTLEMEN, AND PRIESTS; LORD MAYOR OF LONDON AND ALDERMEN; VERGERS, SCRIBES, GUARDS, ATTENDANTS, SERVANTS, AND COMMON PEOPLE; WOMEN ATTENDING UPON QUEEN KATHERINE

SCENE: *London; Kimbolton*]

*

# The Life of King Henry the Eighth

## THE PROLOGUE

**Pro.**

I come no more to make you laugh. Things now
That bear a weighty and a serious brow,
Sad, high, and working, full of state and woe,                    3
Such noble scenes as draw the eye to flow
We now present. Those that can pity, here
May (if they think it well) let fall a tear:
The subject will deserve it. Such as give
Their money out of hope they may believe,
May here find truth too. Those that come to see
Only a show or two and so agree                                   10
The play may pass – if they be still and willing,
I'll undertake may see away their shilling                        12
Richly in two short hours. Only they                              13
That come to hear a merry bawdy play,                             14

---

**Prologue**  3 *Sad . . . working* serious, lofty, and moving; *state* stateliness,
high matters  10 *show* scene  12 *shilling* coin paid for an expensive seat
close to the stage  13 *two . . . hours* (a round number, not the exact running
time of *Henry VIII*)  14 *merry . . . play* (possible allusion to an earlier Henry
VIII play by William Rowley [1605], which included clowns and onstage
fighting)

15  A noise of targets, or to see a fellow
16  In a long motley coat guarded with yellow,
17  Will be deceived. For, gentle hearers, know
    To rank our chosen truth with such a show
19  As fool and fight is, beside forfeiting
20  Our own brains and the opinion that we bring
21  To make that only true we now intend,
22  Will leave us never an understanding friend.
    Therefore, for goodness' sake, and as you are known
24  The first and happiest hearers of the town,
25  Be sad, as we would make ye. Think ye see
    The very persons of our noble story
    As they were living. Think you see them great,
    And followed with the general throng and sweat
    Of thousand friends. Then, in a moment, see
30  How soon this mightiness meets misery.
    And if you can be merry then, I'll say
    A man may weep upon his wedding day.

                    *

∾ **I.1** *Enter the Duke of Norfolk at one door; at*
   *the other, the Duke of Buckingham and the Lord*
   *Abergavenny.*

BUCKINGHAM
  Good morrow and well met. How have ye done
  Since last we saw in France?

---

15 *targets* shields (here, being struck)   16 *motley coat* particolored garb of a
jester; *guarded* trimmed   17 *deceived* disappointed   19–20 *forfeiting . . .
brains* (1) abandoning all claims to intelligence, (2) squandering our intellec-
tual effort   20 *opinion* intent, disposition   21 *make . . . intend* i.e., make
the work we propose true to the historical facts   22 *understanding* (play on
"understanders," the "groundlings" who, for lower admission prices, watched
the play standing around the stage)   24 *happiest* most fortunate   25 *sad* serious
   I.1 London, the royal palace

NORFOLK                               I thank your grace,
  Healthful, and ever since a fresh admirer                                3
  Of what I saw there.                                                      4
BUCKINGHAM           An untimely ague
  Stayed me a prisoner in my chamber when
  Those suns of glory, those two lights of men,                             6
  Met in the vale of Andren.                                                7
NORFOLK                               'Twixt Guynes and Arde.
  I was then present, saw them salute on horseback,
  Beheld them when they lighted, how they clung                             9
  In their embracement, as they grew together;                             10
  Which had they, what four throned ones could have                        11
    weighed
  Such a compounded one?
BUCKINGHAM                       All the whole time
  I was my chamber's prisoner.
NORFOLK                               Then you lost
  The view of earthly glory. Men might say
  Till this time pomp was single, but now married                          15
  To one above itself. Each following day
  Became the next day's master, till the last                              17
  Made former wonders, its. Today the French,                              18
  All clinquant, all in gold, like heathen gods                            19
  Shone down the English; and tomorrow they                                20
  Made Britain India: every man that stood                                 21
  Showed like a mine. Their dwarfish pages were                            22
  As cherubins, all gilt. The madams too,                                  23
  Not used to toil, did almost sweat to bear

---

3 *fresh* undimmed   4 *ague* fever   6 *Those . . . men* i.e., Henry VIII and
Francis I of France   7 *Guynes . . . Arde* i.e., Guines and Ardres, in Picardy
9 *lighted* alighted   10 *as* as if   11 *weighed* equaled in weight   15–16
*pomp . . . itself* i.e., the united pomp of the two kings took pomp itself to a
higher level, as if it had married up   17 *master* teacher   18 *Made . . . its* ab-
sorbed all the glories of the previous days   19 *clinquant* glittering   21 *India*
i.e., the West Indies   22 *Showed* appeared   23 *madams* ladies of rank

25  The pride upon them, that their very labor
26  Was to them as a painting. Now this masque
27  Was cried incomparable; and th' ensuing night
    Made it a fool and beggar. The two kings,
    Equal in luster, were now best, now worst,
30  As presence did present them: him in eye
    Still him in praise; and being present both,
32  'Twas said they saw but one, and no discerner
33  Durst wag his tongue in censure. When these suns
34  (For so they phrase 'em) by their heralds challenged
    The noble spirits to arms, they did perform
36  Beyond thought's compass, that former fabulous story,
    Being now seen possible enough, got credit,
38  That Bevis was believed.

BUCKINGHAM                        O you go far.

NORFOLK
39  As I belong to worship and affect
40  In honor honesty, the tract of ev'ry thing
41  Would by a good discourser lose some life
    Which action's self was tongue to. All was royal.
43  To the disposing of it nought rebelled;
44  Order gave each thing view. The office did
    Distinctly his full function. Who did guide,
    I mean who set the body and the limbs
47  Of this great sport together? As you guess:
48  One, certes, that promises no element

---

25 *pride* splendid attire   26 *Was . . . painting* i.e., made them flush as if they were wearing cosmetics; *masque* pageant   27 *cried* proclaimed   30–31 *him . . . praise* the one in view was the one praised   32 *saw . . . one* i.e., both appeared alike in majesty; *discerner* onlooker   33 *censure* judgment   34 *phrase* call   36 *that* so that   38 *Bevis* Bevis of Southampton (a legendary hero of ballads and romances)   39 *worship* nobility   39–40 *affect . . . honesty* love and pursue truth for my honor   40 *tract* course   41–42 *Would . . . to* i.e., the action spoke for itself more eloquently than even a good storyteller could convey   43 *disposing* arrangement   44–45 *The office . . . function* each official performed his role perfectly   47 *sport* entertainment   48 *certes* certainly; *promises no element* i.e., you wouldn't expect to be taking part

In such a business.

BUCKINGHAM            I pray you who, my lord?

NORFOLK

All this was ordered by the good discretion                    50
Of the right reverend Cardinal of York.                        51

BUCKINGHAM

The devil speed him! No man's pie is freed
From his ambitious finger. What had he
To do in these fierce vanities? I wonder                        54
That such a keech can with his very bulk                        55
Take up the rays o' th' beneficial sun                          56
And keep it from the earth.

NORFOLK                        Surely, sir,
There's in him stuff that puts him to these ends;
For, being not propped by ancestry, whose grace
Chalks successors their way, nor called upon                    60
For high feats done to th' crown, neither allied               61
To eminent assistants, but spiderlike                          62
Out of his self-drawing web, a gives us note,                  63
The force of his own merit makes his way,                      64
A gift that heaven gives for him, which buys                    65
A place next to the king.

ABERGAVENNY                    I cannot tell
What heaven hath given him. Let some graver eye
Pierce into that; but I can see his pride
Peep through each part of him. Whence has he that?
If not from hell the devil is a niggard,                        70
Or has given all before, and he begins                         71

---

51 *Cardinal of York* i.e., Cardinal Wolsey, who had been born a butcher's
son, and was not a member of the nobility   54 *fierce vanities* (1) extravagant
shows, (2) entertainments of the aggressively powerful and ambitious   55
*keech* lump of fat   56 *Take up* block out; *sun* i.e., the king   60 *Chalks* marks
out   61 *to th' crown* for king and country   62 *assistants* (1) public officials,
(2) powerful associates   63 *self-drawing* spun out of himself; *a . . . note* he
lets it be known   64 *makes his way* wins advancement   65 *for him* on his be-
half   70 *niggard* grudging hoarder   71–72 *he begins . . . himself* i.e., the
devil having given him all his pride, Wolsey has begun a new hell himself

A new hell in himself.

BUCKINGHAM                         Why the devil,

73   Upon this French going out, took he upon him
74   (Without the privity o' th' king) t' appoint
75   Who should attend on him? He makes up the file
     Of all the gentry, for the most part such
77   To whom as great a charge as little honor
78   He meant to lay upon; and his own letter,
     The honorable board of council out,
80   Must fetch him in he papers.

ABERGAVENNY                         I do know
     Kinsmen of mine, three at the least, that have
82   By this so sickened their estates that never
     They shall abound as formerly.

BUCKINGHAM                         O many
84   Have broke their backs with laying manors on 'em
     For this great journey. What did this vanity
86   But minister communication of
     A most poor issue?

NORFOLK                         Grievingly I think
88   The peace between the French and us not values
     The cost that did conclude it.

BUCKINGHAM                         Every man,
90   After the hideous storm that followed, was
91   A thing inspired, and not consulting broke
     Into a general prophecy: that this tempest,
93   Dashing the garment of this peace, aboded

---

73 *going out* expedition  74 *the privity* making the king privy to his inten-
tions  75 *file* list  77–78 *To whom . . . upon* i.e., whom he meant to tax rather
than honor  78–80 *his . . . papers* i.e., he may summon ("paper") whomever
he wishes without consulting the council  82 *sickened* impoverished  84
*Have . . . 'em* i.e., have ruined themselves by spending whole manors' worth
on their wardrobes  86 *minister communication* give occasion for talk  88
*not values* isn't worth  90 *the hideous storm* (an actual storm that, according
to the chroniclers, interrupted the proceedings on June 18)  91 *thing inspired* prophet  91–92 *not consulting . . . prophecy* i.e., was taken as a
prophecy even without any consultation  93 *aboded* boded

The sudden breach on't. 94
NORFOLK  Which is budded out;
For France hath flawed the league and hath attached 95
Our merchants' goods at Bordeaux.
ABERGAVENNY  Is it therefore
Th' ambassador is silenced? 97
NORFOLK  Marry is't!
ABERGAVENNY
A proper title of a peace, and purchased 98
At a superfluous rate! 99
BUCKINGHAM  Why, all this business
Our reverend cardinal carried. 100
NORFOLK  Like it your grace,
The state takes notice of the private difference 101
Betwixt you and the cardinal. I advise you
(And take it from a heart that wishes towards you
Honor and plenteous safety) that you read 104
The cardinal's malice and his potency
Together; to consider further, that
What his high hatred would effect wants not 107
A minister in his power. You know his nature, 108
That he's revengeful; and I know his sword
Hath a sharp edge; it's long, and 't may be said *110*
It reaches far, and where 'twill not extend
Thither he darts it. Bosom up my counsel; 112
You'll find it wholesome. Lo where comes that rock

---

94 *sudden . . . on't* imminent breach of the peace  95 *flawed* broken; *attached* seized  97 *silenced* i.e., the French ambassador has been confined to his quarters (reported in Hall's chronicle); *Marry* (an exclamation – a mild oath, originally on the name of the Virgin Mary)  98 *A . . . peace* A fine thing to call a peace!  99 *superfluous* extravagant  100 *Like it* if it please  101 *difference* quarrel  104 *read* consider  107 *wants not* doesn't lack  108 *minister* agent  112 *darts it* i.e., shoots an arrow; *Bosom up* hide in your bosom

114    That I advise your shunning.
       *Enter Cardinal Wolsey, the purse borne before him,*
       *certain of the Guard, and two Secretaries with papers.*
       *The Cardinal in his passage fixeth his eye on*
       *Buckingham, and Buckingham on him, both full*
       *of disdain.*

WOLSEY
115    The Duke of Buckingham's surveyor, ha?
116    Where's his examination?

FIRST SECRETARY        Here, so please you.

WOLSEY
    Is he in person ready?

FIRST SECRETARY        Ay, please your grace.

WOLSEY
    Well, we shall then know more, and Buckingham
119    Shall lessen this big look. *Exeunt Cardinal and his train.*

BUCKINGHAM
120    This butcher's cur is venom-mouthed, and I
    Have not the power to muzzle him; therefore best
122    Not wake him in his slumber. A beggar's book
123    Outworths a noble's blood.

NORFOLK        What, are you chafed?
124    Ask God for temp'rance. That's th' appliance only
    Which your disease requires.

BUCKINGHAM        I read in's looks
    Matter against me, and his eye reviled
    Me as his abject object. At this instant
128    He bores me with some trick. He's gone to th' king.
    I'll follow and outstare him.

NORFOLK        Stay, my lord,
130    And let your reason with your choler question
    What 'tis you go about. To climb steep hills

---

114 s.d. *purse* bag containing the great seal, emblem of the Lord Chancellor's office  115 *surveyor* estate overseer  116 *examination* paper containing the witness's deposition  119 *big look* haughty expression  122 *book* learning 123 *chafed* angered  124 *appliance* remedy  128 *bores* cheats  130 *choler* rage

Requires slow pace at first. Anger is like
A full hot horse, who being allowed his way,
Self-mettle tires him. Not a man in England                        134
Can advise me like you. Be to yourself
As you would to your friend.

BUCKINGHAM                      I'll to the king
And from a mouth of honor quite cry down
This Ipswich fellow's insolence, or proclaim                        138
There's difference in no persons.                                   139

NORFOLK                          Be advised.
Heat not a furnace for your foe so hot                              140
That it do singe yourself. We may outrun
By violent swiftness that which we run at,
And lose by overrunning. Know you not
The fire that mounts the liquor till't run o'er                     144
In seeming to augment it wastes it? Be advised.
I say again there is no English soul
More stronger to direct you than yourself,
If with the sap of reason you would quench,
Or but allay the fire of passion.                                  149

BUCKINGHAM                      Sir,
I am thankful to you, and I'll go along                             150
By your prescription. But this top-proud fellow –                  151
Whom from the flow of gall I name not, but                         152
From sincere motions – by intelligence,                            153
And proofs as clear as founts in July when
We see each grain of gravel, I do know
To be corrupt and treasonous.

NORFOLK                          Say not treasonous.

BUCKINGHAM
To th' king I'll say't and make my vouch as strong                 157

---

134 *Self-mettle* his own ardor   138 *Ipswich* (Wolsey's humble birthplace, a
village in the London orbit)   139 *There's difference . . . no persons* differences
of rank don't exist; *Be advised* take care   144 *mounts the liquor* causes the
fluid to rise   149 *allay* temper   151 *prescription* advice   152–53 *Whom . . .
motions* whom I mention, not out of anger, but with sincere motives   153
*intelligence* secret information   157 *vouch* attestation

As shore of rock. Attend. This holy fox,
Or wolf, or both (for he is equal rav'nous
160     As he is subtile, and as prone to mischief
161     As able to perform't), his mind and place
Infecting one another, yea reciprocally,
Only to show his pomp as well in France
164     As here at home, suggests the king our master
To this last costly treaty; th' interview
That swallowed so much treasure and like a glass
167     Did break i' th' wrenching.

NORFOLK                              Faith, and so it did.

BUCKINGHAM
Pray give me favor, sir. This cunning cardinal
169     The articles o' th' combination drew
170     As himself pleased; and they were ratified
As he cried "Thus let be," to as much end
172     As give a crutch to th' dead. But our count-cardinal
Has done this, and 'tis well; for worthy Wolsey
(Who cannot err) he did it. Now this follows
(Which, as I take it, is a kind of puppy
176     To th' old dam, treason), Charles the emperor,
Under pretense to see the queen his aunt
178     (For 'twas indeed his color, but he came
To whisper Wolsey), here makes visitation.
180     His fears were that the interview betwixt
England and France might through their amity
182     Breed him some prejudice, for from this league
Peeped harms that menaced him: privily
184     Deals with our cardinal, and, as I trow,
Which I do well; for I am sure the emperor
Paid ere he promised, whereby his suit was granted
Ere it was asked; but when the way was made,

---

**161** *place* office   **164** *suggests* inveigles, prompts   **167** *wrenching* (1) rinsing, (2) rough handling   **169** *combination* pact   **172** *count-cardinal* i.e., upstart cardinal behaving like a nobleman   **176** *dam* mother (i.e., of the *puppy*) **178** *color* pretext   **182** *Breed . . . prejudice* work to his disadvantage   **184** *trow* believe

And paved with gold, the emperor thus desired,
That he would please to alter the king's course
And break the foresaid peace. Let the king know          *190*
(As soon he shall by me) that thus the cardinal
Does buy and sell his honor as he pleases,
And for his own advantage.

NORFOLK                              I am sorry
To hear this of him, and could wish he were
Something mistaken in't.                                 195

BUCKINGHAM                     No, not a syllable.
I do pronounce him in that very shape                    196
He shall appear in proof.                                197

        *Enter Brandon, a Sergeant at Arms before him, and*
        *two or three of the Guard.*

BRANDON
Your office, sergeant; execute it.

SERGEANT                              Sir,
My lord the Duke of Buckingham, and Earl
Of Hereford, Stafford, and Northampton, I               *200*
Arrest thee of high treason, in the name
Of our most sovereign king.                              202

BUCKINGHAM                     Lo you, my lord,
The net has fall'n upon me! I shall perish
Under device and practice.                               204

BRANDON                        I am sorry
To see you ta'en from liberty, to look on               205
The business present. 'Tis his highness' pleasure
You shall to th' Tower.

BUCKINGHAM               It will help me nothing
To plead mine innocence, for that dye is on me
Which makes my whit'st part black. The will of heav'n
Be done in this and all things! I obey.                  *210*
O my Lord Aberga'ny, fare you well!

---

195 *Something mistaken* somewhat misperceived  196 *pronounce* make
known  197 *in proof* (1) in experience, (2) when exposed  202 *Lo* look
204 *device and practice* stratagem and plot  205 *look on* be a witness of

BRANDON
    Nay, he must bear you company.
        *[To Abergavenny]*            The king
    Is pleased you shall to th' Tower till you know
    How he determines further.
ABERGAVENNY                    As the duke said,
    The will of heaven be done, and the king's pleasure
    By me obeyed!
BRANDON          Here is a warrant from
217    The king t' attach Lord Montacute and the bodies
    Of the duke's confessor, John de la Car,
    One Gilbert Perk, his chancellor –
BUCKINGHAM                         So, so!
220    These are the limbs o' th' plot. No more, I hope.
BRANDON
    A monk o' th' Chartreux.
BUCKINGHAM                    O, Michael Hopkins?
BRANDON                                    He.
BUCKINGHAM
    My surveyor is false. The o'ergreat cardinal
223    Hath showed him gold; my life is spanned already.
    I am the shadow of poor Buckingham,
225    Whose figure even this instant cloud puts on
    By dark'ning my clear sun. My lord, farewell.    *Exeunt.*

                            ✳

∾ **I.2** *Cornets. Enter King Henry, leaning on the Cardi-*
    *nal's shoulder, the Nobles, [the Cardinal's Secretary,]*
    *and Sir Thomas Lovell. The Cardinal places himself*
    *under the King's feet on his right side.*


KING
1    My life itself, and the best heart of it,

---

217 *attach* arrest   223 *spanned* measured out   225 *cloud puts on* is becoming clouded
    **I.2** The council chamber   1 *best heart* very essence

Thanks you for this great care. I stood i' th' level                    2
Of a full-charged confederacy, and give thanks                        3
To you that choked it. Let be called before us
That gentleman of Buckingham's; in person
I'll hear him his confessions justify,                                 6
And point by point the treasons of his master
He shall again relate.                                                 8
    *A noise within, crying "Room for the Queen!" Enter*
    *the Queen, ushered by the Duke of Norfolk, and*
    *Suffolk. She kneels. [The] King riseth from his state,*
    *takes her up, kisses and placeth her by him.*

KATHERINE
Nay, we must longer kneel. I am a suitor.

KING
Arise and take place by us. Half your suit                            10
Never name to us; you have half our power.
The other moiety ere you ask is given.                                12
Repeat your will, and take it.                                        13

KATHERINE                                Thank your majesty.
That you would love yourself, and in that love
Not unconsidered leave your honor nor
The dignity of your office, is the point
Of my petition.

KING                          Lady mine, proceed.

KATHERINE
I am solicited, not by a few,
And those of true condition, that your subjects                       19
Are in great grievance. There have been commissions                  20
Sent down among 'em, which hath flawed the heart                      21
Of all their loyalties; wherein, although,
My good lord cardinal, they vent reproaches
Most bitterly on you as putter-on

---

2 *level* line of fire   3 *full-charged* fully loaded; *confederacy* conspiracy   6 *jus-*
*tify* confirm   8 **s.d.** *state* throne   12 *moiety* portion   13 *Repeat* state   19
*true condition* loyal disposition   20 *grievance* distress; *commissions* tax writs
21 *flawed* broken

Of these exactions, yet the king our master –

26    Whose honor heaven shield from soil! – even he escapes not

27    Language unmannerly; yea such which breaks
The sides of loyalty and almost appears
In loud rebellion.

NORFOLK          Not almost appears –

30    It doth appear. For upon these taxations,
The clothiers all not able to maintain

32    The many to them longing, have put off

33    The spinsters, carders, fullers, weavers, who,
Unfit for other life, compelled by hunger
And lack of other means, in desperate manner

36    Daring th' event to th' teeth, are all in uproar,

37    And danger serves among them.

KING                 Taxation?
Wherein? And what taxation? My lord cardinal,
You that are blamed for it alike with us,

40    Know you of this taxation?

WOLSEY            Please you, sir,

41    I know but of a single part in aught

42    Pertains to th' state, and front but in that file

43    Where others tell steps with me.

KATHERINE         No, my lord?

44    You know no more than others? But you frame

45    Things that are known alike, which are not wholesome

46    To those which would not know them and yet must

47    Perforce be their acquaintance. These exactions

---

26 *soil* taint   27–28 *breaks / The sides* ruptures the bounds   32 *longing* belonging (i.e., employees dependent upon them)   33 *spinsters* spinners; *carders* those who comb the wool for impurities; *fullers* those who beat the wool to clean and mat it   36 *Daring . . . to th' teeth* i.e., defiantly accepting the risks of revolt   37 *danger . . . among them* i.e., they accept danger but also threaten mischief   41 *a single part* one person's share   42 *front . . . file* march in the front rank   43 *tell steps* march in step   44 *frame* shape, instigate   45 *known alike* known to all (in council)   46 *would not know* don't want to know   47 *exactions* onerous requirements

(Whereof my sovereign would have note) they are            48
Most pestilent to th' hearing; and, to bear 'em,
The back is sacrifice to th' load. They say              50
They are devised by you, or else you suffer
Too hard an exclamation.                        52

KING                            Still exaction!
The nature of it? In what kind, let's know,              53
Is this exaction?

KATHERINE         I am much too venturous
In tempting of your patience, but am boldened
Under your promised pardon. The subject's grief          56
Comes through commissions, which compels from
    each
The sixth part of his substance, to be levied
Without delay; and the pretense for this
Is named, your wars in France. This makes bold    60
    mouths.
Tongues spit their duties out, and cold hearts freeze
Allegiance in them. Their curses now
Live where their prayers did; and it's come to pass
This tractable obedience is a slave                  64
To each incensèd will. I would your highness        65
Would give it quick consideration, for
There is no primer business.                      67

KING                          By my life,
This is against our pleasure.

WOLSEY                          And for me,
I have no further gone in this than by
A single voice, and that not passed me but          70
By learned approbation of the judges. If I am
Traduced by ignorant tongues, which neither know    72
My faculties nor person yet will be               73

---

48 *note* knowledge   50 *is sacrifice* becomes a sacrifice   52 *exclamation* out-
cry, reproach   53 *kind* form   56 *grief* grievance   64 *tractable* docile   65
*each incensèd will* each individual's outraged passion   67 *primer* more urgent
70 *single voice* unanimous vote; *passed me* approved by me   72 *Traduced*
slandered   73 *faculties* qualities

The chronicles of my doing, let me say
75 'Tis but the fate of place and the rough brake
76 That virtue must go through. We must not stint
Our necessary actions in the fear
78 To cope malicious censurers, which ever,
As rav'nous fishes, do a vessel follow
80 That is new-trimmed, but benefit no further
Than vainly longing. What we oft do best,
82 By sick interpreters (once weak ones) is
83 Not ours, or not allowed; what worst, as oft
84 Hitting a grosser quality, is cried up
For our best act. If we shall stand still,
86 In fear our motion will be mocked or carped at,
We should take root here where we sit,
88 Or sit state-statues only.

KING                                    Things done well
And with a care exempt themselves from fear;
90 Things done without example, in their issue
Are to be feared. Have you a precedent
Of this commission? I believe, not any.
93 We must not rend our subjects from our laws
94 And stick them in our will. Sixth part of each?
95 A trembling contribution! Why, we take
96 From every tree lop, bark, and part o' th' timber;
And though we leave it with a root, thus hacked,
The air will drink the sap. To every county
Where this is questioned, send our letters with
100 Free pardon to each man that has denied
101 The force of this commission. Pray look to't.

---

75 *place* high office; *brake* thicket  76 *stint* cease to do  78 *cope* encounter
80 *new-trimmed* newly fitted  82 *sick* envious, malicious  83 *Not ours* not
credited to us; *allowed* approved  84 *Hitting . . . quality* appealing to the (ignorant) masses  86 *motion* (1) movement, (2) proposal  88 *state-statues* i.e.,
mere statues of statesmen  90 *example* legitimizing precedent; *issue* outcome
93 *rend* tear (away)  94 *stick . . . will* i.e., make them subject only to our
capricious will  95 *trembling* fearful  96 *lop* the crown of the tree  101
*force* lawful authority

I put it to your care.
WOLSEY   *[Aside to the Secretary]*
                   A word with you.
 Let there be letters writ to every shire
Of the king's grace and pardon. The grievèd commons    104
Hardly conceive of me. Let it be noised    105
That through our intercession this revokement
And pardon comes. I shall anon advise you
Further in the proceeding.         *Exit Secretary.*
   *Enter Surveyor.*
KATHERINE
 I am sorry that the Duke of Buckingham
Is run in your displeasure.    110
KING                  It grieves many.
 The gentleman is learned and a most rare speaker,
To nature none more bound; his training such    112
That he may furnish and instruct great teachers
And never seek for aid out of himself. Yet see,    114
When these so noble benefits shall prove
Not well disposed, the mind growing once corrupt,    116
They turn to vicious forms, ten times more ugly    117
Than ever they were fair. This man so complete,    118
Who was enrolled 'mongst wonders – and when we,
Almost with ravished list'ning, could not find    *120*
His hour of speech a minute – he, my lady,
Hath into monstrous habits put the graces    122
That once were his, and is become as black
As if besmeared in hell. Sit by us. You shall hear
(This was his gentleman in trust) of him
Things to strike honor sad. Bid him recount
The fore-recited practices, whereof    127
We cannot feel too little, hear too much.

---

**104** *grace* mercy  **105** *Hardly conceive* think harshly; *noised* rumored  **110** *Is run in* has incurred  **112** *bound* indebted  **114** *out of* outside of  **116** *disposed* directed  **117** *vicious* evil  **118** *complete* accomplished  **122** *habits* costumes (i.e., guises)  **127** *practices* intrigues

WOLSEY

    Stand forth, and with bold spirit relate what you
130    Most like a careful subject have collected
    Out of the Duke of Buckingham.

KING                                Speak freely.

SURVEYOR

    First, it was usual with him – every day
    It would infect his speech – that if the king
134    Should without issue die, he'll carry it so
    To make the scepter his. These very words
    I've heard him utter to his son-in-law,
    Lord Aberga'ny, to whom by oath he menaced
    Revenge upon the cardinal.

WOLSEY                   Please your highness note
    This dangerous conception in this point:
140    Not friended by his wish to your high person,
    His will is most malignant, and it stretches
    Beyond you to your friends.

KATHERINE               My learned lord cardinal,
143    Deliver all with charity.

KING                  Speak on.
    How grounded he his title to the crown
145    Upon our fail? To this point hast thou heard him
    At any time speak aught?

SURVEYOR            He was brought to this
147    By a vain prophecy of Nicholas Henton.

KING

    What was that Henton?

SURVEYOR            Sir, a Chartreux friar,
    His confessor, who fed him every minute
150    With words of sovereignty.

KING                 How know'st thou this?

---

130–31 *collected/Out of* gathered from or about   134 *issue* progeny; *carry it so* contrive   140 *friended by* gratified in (i.e., the wish that the king will die without an heir)   143 *Deliver* relate   145 *fail* (1) death, (2) failure to produce an heir   147 *Henton* (otherwise Michael Hopkins; see I.1.221)

SURVEYOR
    Not long before your highness sped to France,
    The duke being at the Rose, within the parish         152
    Saint Lawrence Poultney, did of me demand
    What was the speech among the Londoners
    Concerning the French journey. I replied,
    Men feared the French would prove perfidious,
    To the king's danger. Presently the duke           157
    Said 'twas the fear indeed, and that he doubted      158
    'Twould prove the verity of certain words
    Spoke by a holy monk "that oft," says he,          *160*
    "Hath sent to me, wishing me to permit
    John de la Car, my chaplain, a choice hour
    To hear from him a matter of some moment;
    Whom after under the confession's seal
    He solemnly had sworn that what he spoke
    My chaplain to no creature living but
    To me should utter, with demure confidence       167
    This pausingly ensued: neither the king nor's heirs  168
    (Tell you the duke) shall prosper. Bid him strive
    To [win] the love o' th' commonalty. The duke    170
    Shall govern England."
KATHERINE              If I know you well,
    You were the duke's surveyor and lost your office
    On the complaint o' th' tenants. Take good heed
    You charge not in your spleen a noble person     174
    And spoil your nobler soul. I say, take heed;      175
    Yes, heartily beseech you.
KING                Let him on.
    Go forward.
SURVEYOR      On my soul, I'll speak but truth.
    I told my lord the duke, by th' devil's illusions    178

---

152 *Rose* i.e., Manor of the Red Rose, belonging to Buckingham  157
*Presently* immediately  158 *doubted* feared  167 *demure confidence* solemn
conviction  168 *pausingly* with pauses between words  170 *commonalty*
common people  174 *spleen* malice  175 *spoil* ruin  178 *illusions* decep-
tions

The monk might be deceived; and that 'twas dangerous
180   To ruminate on this so far until
181   It forged him some design, which, being believed,
182   It was much like to do. He answered, "Tush,
It can do me no damage!" adding further
184   That, had the king in his last sickness failed,
The cardinal's and Sir Thomas Lovell's heads
186   Should have gone off.

KING                 Ha! What, so rank? Ah, ha!
There's mischief in this man. Canst thou say further?

SURVEYOR
I can, my liege.

KING         Proceed.

SURVEYOR            Being at Greenwich,
After your highness had reproved the duke
190   About Sir William Bulmer –

KING                   I remember
Of such a time. Being my sworn servant,
The duke retained him his. But on: what hence?

SURVEYOR
"If," quoth he, "I for this had been committed,
As to the Tower I thought, I would have played
The part my father meant to act upon
196   Th' usurper Richard, who, being at Salisbury,
Made suit to come in's presence, which if granted,
198   As he made semblance of his duty, would
Have put his knife into him."

KING                A giant traitor!

WOLSEY
200   Now, madam, may his highness live in freedom,
And this man out of prison?

KATHERINE          God mend all.

---

181 *forged* shaped   182 *to do* i.e., to bring him into danger   184 *failed* died
186 *rank* (1) grossly corrupt, (2) rebellious   196 *Th' usurper Richard* i.e.,
Richard III (cf. Shakespeare's play so titled)   198 *made semblance . . . duty*
feigned homage

KING
    There's something more would out of thee. What say'st?
SURVEYOR
    After "the duke his father," with the "knife,"
    He stretched him, and, with one hand on his dagger,    204
    Another spread on's breast, mounting his eyes,    205
    He did discharge a horrible oath, whose tenor
    Was, were he evil used, he would outgo    207
    His father by as much as a performance
    Does an irresolute purpose.    209
KING                    There's his period,
    To sheathe his knife in us. He is attached;    210
    Call him to present trial. If he may    211
    Find mercy in the law, 'tis his: if none,
    Let him not seek't of us. By day and night,
    He's traitor to th' height!           *Exeunt.*    214

*

∾ **I.3** *Enter Lord Chamberlain and Lord Sandys.*

CHAMBERLAIN
    Is't possible the spells of France should juggle    1
    Men into such strange mysteries?    2
SANDYS                 New customs,
    Though they be never so ridiculous
    (Nay, let 'em be unmanly), yet are followed.
CHAMBERLAIN
    As far as I see, all the good our English
    Have got by the late voyage is but merely
    A fit or two o' th' face; but they are shrewd ones,    7
    For when they hold 'em, you would swear directly    8

---

**204** *stretched him* drew himself up  **205** *mounting* raising  **207** *evil used*
mistreated  **209** *period* goal, conclusion  **210** *attached* arrested  **211** *present* immediate  **214** *to th' height* in the highest degree

    **I.3** The royal palace  **1** *juggle* trick  **2** *strange mysteries* i.e., bizarre fashions
**7** *A fit . . . face* i.e., odd grimaces  **8** *hold 'em* i.e., keep their expressions fixed

Their very noses had been counselors
10    To Pepin or Clotharius, they keep state so.

SANDYS
11    They have all new legs, and lame ones. One would take
     it,
12    That never see 'em pace before, the spavin,
13    A springhalt reigned among 'em.

CHAMBERLAIN                    Death my lord,
14    Their clothes are after such a pagan cut to't
     That sure th' have worn out Christendom.

      *Enter Sir Thomas Lovell.*          How now?
     What news, Sir Thomas Lovell?

LOVELL                   Faith, my lord,
     I hear of none but the new proclamation
     That's clapped upon the court gate.

CHAMBERLAIN              What is't for?

LOVELL
     The reformation of our traveled gallants
20    That fill the court with quarrels, talk, and tailors.

CHAMBERLAIN
     I'm glad 'tis there. Now I would pray our monsieurs
     To think an English courtier may be wise
     And never see the Louvre.

LOVELL            They must either
     (For so run the conditions) leave those remnants
25    Of fool and feather that they got in France,
26    With all their honorable points of ignorance
27    Pertaining thereunto – as fights and fireworks;
     Abusing better men than they can be,

---

10 *Pepin, Clotharius* early kings of France; *keep state* maintain their loftiness
11 *legs* ways of walking and/or bowing (making a leg)    12 *pace* strut; *spavin*
tumor on the leg of a horse    13 *springhalt* crippling ailment of a horse's
sinews    14 *to't* furthermore    25 *fool and feather* (folly and extravagant feath-
ers are connected here)    26 *honorable . . . ignorance* points they ignorantly
regard as ones of honor    27 *fights and fireworks* mock battles and fireworks
displays ( *fireworks* possibly alluding to whoring as well)

Out of a foreign wisdom – renouncing clean                    29
The faith they have in tennis and tall stockings,             30
Short blistered breeches, and those types of travel,          31
And understand again like honest men,
Or pack to their old playfellows. There, I take it,           33
They may *cum privilegio* "wee" away                          34
The lag end of their lewdness and be laughed at.              35

SANDYS
'Tis time to give 'em physic, their diseases
Are grown so catching.

CHAMBERLAIN                      What a loss our ladies
Will have of these trim vanities!                             38

LOVELL                                    Ay, marry,
There will be woe indeed, lords. The sly whoresons           39
Have got a speeding trick to lay down ladies.                40
A French song and a fiddle has no fellow.

SANDYS
The devil fiddle 'em! I am glad they are going,
For sure there's no converting of 'em. Now
An honest country lord, as I am, beaten
A long time out of play, may bring his plain song            45
And have an hour of hearing, and, by'r Lady,                 46
Held current music too.                                       47

CHAMBERLAIN                    Well said, Lord Sandys.
Your colt's tooth is not cast yet?                            48

SANDYS                              No, my lord,
Nor shall not while I have a stump.                           49

CHAMBERLAIN                              Sir Thomas,

---

**29** *Out of* on the strength of   **31** *blistered* puffed-out; *types* tokens   **33** *pack* be sent packing   **34** *cum privilegio* with immunity; *wee* (Englishman's comic pronunciation of *oui*)   **35** *lag end* remainder; *lewdness* (1) ignorance, (2) lasciviousness   **38** *trim vanities* stylish trifles   **39** *whoresons* bastards (colloquial)   **40** *speeding* effective   **45** *play* i.e., sexual action; *plain song* simple tune, alluding to the unadorned melodies of the medieval church   **46** *by'r Lady* (oath on the name of the Virgin Mary)   **47** *current* acceptable, good (as currency)   **48** *colt's tooth* (proverbial for youthful wantonness); *cast* fallen out   **49** *stump* i.e., of a tooth, but implying penis

50      Whither were you agoing?
LOVELL                                    To the cardinal's.
        Your lordship is a guest too.
CHAMBERLAIN                          O, 'tis true;
52      This night he makes a supper, and a great one,
        To many lords and ladies. There will be
        The beauty of this kingdom, I'll assure you.
LOVELL
        That churchman bears a bounteous mind indeed,
        A hand as fruitful as the land that feeds us;
        His dews fall everywhere.
CHAMBERLAIN                       No doubt he's noble.
58      He had a black mouth that said other of him.
SANDYS
59      He may, my lord; has wherewithal. In him
60      Sparing would show a worse sin than ill doctrine.
61      Men of his way should be most liberal;
        They are set here for examples.
CHAMBERLAIN                          True, they are so;
        But few now give so great ones. My barge stays;
        Your lordship shall along. Come, good Sir Thomas,
        We shall be late else; which I would not be,
66      For I was spoke to, with Sir Henry Guilford
67      This night to be comptrollers.
SANDYS                             I am your lordship's.
                                        *Exeunt.*

                              *

52 *makes* gives   58 *black* evil, malignant   59 *He may* he is able to   61 *way* way of life, calling; *liberal* generous   66 *spoke to* asked   67 *comptrollers* stewards

∾ **I.4** *Hautboys. A small table under a state for the*
*Cardinal, a longer table for the guests. Then enter*
*Anne Bullen and divers other Ladies and Gentlemen,*
*as guests at one door; at another door enter Sir Henry*
*Guilford.*

GUILFORD

Ladies, a general welcome from his grace
Salutes ye all. This night he dedicates
To fair content and you. None here, he hopes,
In all this noble bevy, has brought with her                           4
One care abroad. He would have all as merry
As first, good company, good wine, good welcome    6
Can make good people.
    *Enter Lord Chamberlain, Lord Sandys, and Lovell.*
                O my lord, you're tardy!
The very thought of this fair company
Clapped wings to me.
CHAMBERLAIN         You are young, Sir Harry Guilford.
SANDYS

Sir Thomas Lovell, had the cardinal                                   *10*
But half my lay thoughts in him, some of these      11
Should find a running banquet ere they rested,      12
I think would better please 'em. By my life,
They are a sweet society of fair ones.
LOVELL

O that your lordship were but now confessor
To one or two of these!
SANDYS               I would I were.
They should find easy penance.
LOVELL                  Faith, how easy?

---

I.4 York Place **s.d.** *Hautboys* oboelike instruments (play); *state* chair of state
4 *bevy* company (ladies emphasized)  6 *As first* i.e., first . . . then . . . then
11 *lay* secular  12 *running* speedy (sexually eyeing the ladies; the joke continues through l. 18, with additional innuendo of spanking)

SANDYS
      As easy as a down bed would afford it.

CHAMBERLAIN
      Sweet ladies, will it please you sit? Sir Harry,
20    Place you that side; I'll take the charge of this.
      His grace is ent'ring. Nay, you must not freeze!
      Two women placed together makes cold weather.
      My Lord Sandys, you are one will keep 'em waking.
      Pray sit between these ladies.

SANDYS                              By my faith,
      And thank your lordship. By your leave, sweet ladies,
          *[Seats himself between Anne Bullen and another lady.]*
      If I chance to talk a little wild, forgive me;
      I had it from my father.

ANNE                          Was he mad, sir?

SANDYS
      O very mad, exceeding mad, in love too.
      But he would bite none. Just as I do now,
30    He would kiss you twenty with a breath.
          *[Kisses her.]*

CHAMBERLAIN                          Well said, my lord.
31    So now you're fairly seated. Gentlemen,
      The penance lies on you if these fair ladies
33    Pass away frowning.

SANDYS                          For my little cure,
34    Let me alone.
          *Hautboys. Enter Cardinal Wolsey, [attended,] and
          takes his state.*

WOLSEY
      You're welcome, my fair guests. That noble lady
      Or gentleman that is not freely merry
      Is not my friend. This to confirm my welcome;
      And to you all, good health.

---

**20** *Place you* you assign seats   **30** *kiss you* kiss; *Well said* well done   **31** *fairly*
properly   **33** *cure* clerical responsibility (to his "parishioners")   **34** *Let me
alone* i.e., I can handle it; **s.d.** *state* chair of state

*[Drinks.]*

SANDYS                  Your grace is noble.
  Let me have such a bowl may hold my thanks
  And save me so much talking.                     40

WOLSEY                My Lord Sandys,
  I am beholding to you: cheer your neighbors.       41
  Ladies, you are not merry; gentlemen,
  Whose fault is this?

SANDYS           The red wine first must rise
  In their fair cheeks, my lord; then we shall have 'em
  Talk us to silence.                           45

ANNE         You are a merry gamester,
  My Lord Sandys.                           46

SANDYS         Yes, if I make my play.
  Here's to your ladyship, and pledge it, madam,
  For 'tis to such a thing –

ANNE              You cannot show me.

SANDYS
  I told your grace they would talk anon.         49
    *Drum and trumpet. Chambers discharged.*

WOLSEY                   What's that?

CHAMBERLAIN
  Look out there, some of ye.     *[Exit a Servant.]*   50

WOLSEY               What warlike voice,
  And to what end is this? Nay ladies, fear not.
  By all the laws of war you're privileged.        52
    *Enter a Servant.*

CHAMBERLAIN
  How now, what is't?

SERVANT         A noble troop of strangers
  For so they seem. Th' have left their barge and landed,
  And hither make, as great ambassadors

---

41 *beholding* obliged   45 *gamester* joker, player of sexual games   46 *make my play* (1) win, (2) plead my cause   49 s.d. *Chambers* small cannons (which probably set fire to the Globe theater in 1613; see Introduction); *discharged* fired   52 *you're privileged* you have immunity

From foreign princes.

WOLSEY                    Good lord chamberlain,
Go, give 'em welcome; you can speak the French
  tongue.
And pray receive 'em nobly and conduct 'em
Into our presence, where this heaven of beauty
60  Shall shine at full upon them. Some attend him!
                    *[Exit Chamberlain, attended.]*
        *All rise, and tables removed.*
61  You have now a broken banquet, but we'll mend it.
A good digestion to you all, and once more
63  I show'r a welcome on ye: welcome all.
        *Hautboys. Enter King and others, as masquers,*
        *habited like shepherds, ushered by the Lord*
        *Chamberlain. They pass directly before the Cardinal*
        *and gracefully salute him.*
A noble company! What are their pleasures?

CHAMBERLAIN
Because they speak no English, thus they prayed
66  To tell your grace: that having heard by fame
Of this so noble and so fair assembly
This night to meet here, they could do no less
(Out of the great respect they bear to beauty)
70  But leave their flocks and, under your fair conduct,
Crave leave to view these ladies and entreat
An hour of revels with 'em.

WOLSEY                    Say, lord chamberlain,
They have done my poor house grace; for which I pay
  'em
74  A thousand thanks and pray 'em take their pleasures.
        *Choose ladies. King and Anne Bullen.*

KING
The fairest hand I ever touched: O beauty,

---

61 *broken* interrupted   63 s.d. *masquers* masked dancers or performers;
*habited* dressed   66 *fame* report   70 *conduct* guidance   74 s.d. *Choose . . .*
*Bullen* the men choose partners; Henry chooses Anne Bullen

Till now I never knew thee!
  *Music. Dance.*
WOLSEY
  My lord!
CHAMBERLAIN     Your grace?
WOLSEY                         Pray tell 'em thus much from
    me:
  There should be one amongst 'em, by his person,
  More worthy this place than myself; to whom,          79
  If I but knew him, with my love and duty              80
  I would surrender it.
CHAMBERLAIN          I will, my lord.
    *Whisper [with the Masquers].*
WOLSEY
  What say they?
CHAMBERLAIN     Such a one they all confess
  There is indeed, which they would have your grace
  Find out, and he will take it.                        84
WOLSEY                         Let me see then –
  By all your good leaves, gentlemen; here I'll make
  My royal choice.
KING     *[Unmasks.]* Ye have found him, cardinal.
  You hold a fair assembly. You do well, lord.
  You are a churchman, or I'll tell you, cardinal,
  I should judge now unhappily.                         89
WOLSEY                         I am glad
  Your grace is grown so pleasant.                      90
KING                         My lord chamberlain,
  Prithee come hither. What fair lady's that?
CHAMBERLAIN
  An't please your grace, Sir Thomas Bullen's daughter,
  The Viscount Rochford, one of her highness' women.

---

79 *place* position of eminence   84 *Find out* identify; *it* i.e., the place of
honor   89 *unhappily* unfavorably (of his princely display)   90 *pleasant* humorous

KING
    By heaven she is a dainty one. Sweetheart,
95     I were unmannerly to take you out
    And not to kiss you. *[Kisses her.]* A health, gentlemen!
97     Let it go round.
WOLSEY
    Sir Thomas Lovell, is the banquet ready
    I' th' privy chamber?
LOVELL               Yes, my lord.
WOLSEY                    Your grace,
100    I fear, with dancing is a little heated.
KING
    I fear, too much.
WOLSEY          There's fresher air, my lord,
    In the next chamber.
KING
    Lead in your ladies ev'ry one. Sweet partner,
    I must not yet forsake you. Let's be merry,
    Good my lord cardinal. I have half a dozen healths
106    To drink to these fair ladies, and a measure
    To lead 'em once again; and then let's dream
108    Who's best in favor. Let the music knock it.
                             *Exeunt with Trumpets.*

✳

∾ **II.1** *Enter two Gentlemen at several doors.*

FIRST GENTLEMAN
    Whither away so fast?
SECOND GENTLEMAN    O, God save ye!
2     Ev'n to the Hall, to hear what shall become
    Of the great Duke of Buckingham.

---

95 *take you out* lead you out to the dance  97 *it* i.e., the cup  100 *heated*
(implying sexually aroused)  106 *measure* dance  108 *in favor* i.e., (1) with
the ladies, (2) in looks; **s.d.** *knock it* strike up; **s.d.** *Trumpets* trumpeters
    II.1 A street **s.d.** *several* separate  2 *the Hall* Westminster Hall

FIRST GENTLEMAN                          I'll save you
  That labor, sir. All's now done but the ceremony
  Of bringing back the prisoner.
SECOND GENTLEMAN                    Were you there?
FIRST GENTLEMAN
  Yes indeed was I.
SECOND GENTLEMAN
                Pray speak what has happened.
FIRST GENTLEMAN
  You may guess quickly what.
SECOND GENTLEMAN               Is he found guilty?
FIRST GENTLEMAN
  Yes truly is he, and condemned upon't.
SECOND GENTLEMAN
  I am sorry for't.
FIRST GENTLEMAN
          So are a number more.
SECOND GENTLEMAN
  But pray how passed it?                                          10
FIRST GENTLEMAN
  I'll tell you in a little. The great duke                        11
  Came to the bar; where to his accusations
  He pleaded still not guilty, and alleged                          13
  Many sharp reasons to defeat the law.                             14
  The king's attorney, on the contrary,                            15
  Urged on the examinations, proofs, confessions                   16
  Of divers witnesses, which the duke desired
  To him brought *viva voce* to his face;                          18
  At which appeared against him his surveyor,
  Sir Gilbert Perk his chancellor, and John Car,                   20
  Confessor to him, with that devil monk,
  Hopkins, that made this mischief.

---

10 *passed it* did the trial proceed   11 *in a little* briefly   13 *alleged* put forward   14 *sharp reasons* acute arguments   15 *on the contrary* opposing these
arguments   16 *Urged on* pressed as evidence   18 *viva voce* in person (literally, "with living voice")   20 *chancellor* secretary

SECOND GENTLEMAN                    That was he
  That fed him with his prophecies.
FIRST GENTLEMAN                    The same.
24    All these accused him strongly, which he fain
    Would have flung from him, but indeed he could not;
    And so his peers upon this evidence
    Have found him guilty of high treason. Much
    He spoke, and learnedly for life; but all
    Was either pitied in him or forgotten.
SECOND GENTLEMAN
30    After all this how did he bear himself?
FIRST GENTLEMAN
    When he was brought again to th' bar, to hear
32    His knell rung out, his judgment, he was stirred
    With such an agony he sweat extremely
34    And something spoke in choler, ill and hasty;
35    But he fell to himself again, and sweetly
    In all the rest showed a most noble patience.
SECOND GENTLEMAN
  I do not think he fears death.
FIRST GENTLEMAN                    Sure he does not;
  He never was so womanish. The cause
  He may a little grieve at.
SECOND GENTLEMAN          Certainly
40    The cardinal is the end of this.
FIRST GENTLEMAN                    'Tis likely
41    By all conjectures: first Kildare's attendure,
42    Then Deputy of Ireland, who removed,
    Earl Surrey was sent thither, and in haste too,
44    Lest he should help his father.
SECOND GENTLEMAN                    That trick of state
45    Was a deep envious one.

----

24 *fain* wishfully   32 *knell* passing bell; *judgment* sentence   34 *choler* anger
35 *fell to himself* regained self-control   40 *end* cause   41 *attendure* attainder
(confiscation of the earl's estate, upon the death sentence)   42 *Deputy*
viceroy (governor)   44 *father* i.e., father-in-law (Surrey was Buckingham's
son-in-law)   45 *envious* malicious (on Wolsey's part)

FIRST GENTLEMAN                At his return
  No doubt he will requite it. This is noted                    46
  (And generally): whoever the king favors,                     47
  The card'nal instantly will find employment,
  And far enough from court too.

SECOND GENTLEMAN                   All the commons
  Hate him perniciously, and o' my conscience                   50
  Wish him ten fathom deep. This duke as much
  They love and dote on, call him bounteous Bucking-
    ham
  The mirror of all courtesy –                                   53

*Enter Buckingham from his arraignment; Tipstaves*
*before him; [Officer bearing] the [executioner's] ax*
*with the edge towards him; Halberds on each side;*
*accompanied with Sir Thomas Lovell, Sir Nicholas*
*Vaux, Sir Walter Sandys, and common people, etc.*

FIRST GENTLEMAN                Stay there, sir,
  And see the noble ruined man you speak of.

SECOND GENTLEMAN
  Let's stand close and behold him.

BUCKINGHAM                          All good people,
  You that thus far have come to pity me,
  Hear what I say and then go home and lose me.                  57
  I have this day received a traitor's judgment                  58
  And by that name must die. Yet heaven bear witness,
  And if I have a conscience, let it sink me                     60
  Even as the ax falls, if I be not faithful!                    61
  The law I bear no malice for my death,
  'T has done upon the premises but justice;                     63
  But those that sought it I could wish more Christians.
  Be what they will, I heartily forgive 'em.

---

**46** *requite it* pay it back  **47** *generally* by everyone  **50** *perniciously* to the death  **53** *mirror* model; *courtesy* courtly conduct; **s.d.** *Tipstaves* officers who took the accused from court into custody (so called because they carried staves tipped with silver); *Halberds* halberdiers (carrying long-handled battle-axes with spear points)  **57** *lose* forget  **58** *judgment* sentence  **60** *sink* destroy, condemn  **61** *faithful* loyal  **63** *upon the premises* given the evidence

66    Yet let 'em look they glory not in mischief,
67    Nor build their evils on the graves of great men;
      For then my guiltless blood must cry against 'em.
      For further life in this world I ne'er hope,
70    Nor will I sue, although the king have mercies
71    More than I dare make faults. You few that loved me
      And dare be bold to weep for Buckingham,
      His noble friends and fellows, whom to leave
74    Is only bitter to him, only dying,
      Go with me like good angels to my end;
      And, as the long divorce of steel falls on me,
77    Make of your prayers one sweet sacrifice
78    And lift my soul to heaven. Lead on a God's name.

LOVELL
      I do beseech your grace, for charity,
80    If ever any malice in your heart
      Were hid against me, now to forgive me frankly.

BUCKINGHAM
      Sir Thomas Lovell, I as free forgive you
      As I would be forgiven. I forgive all.
      There cannot be those numberless offenses
85    'Gainst me that I cannot take peace with. No black
         envy
      Shall mark my grave. Commend me to his grace;
      And if he speak of Buckingham, pray tell him
      You met him half in heaven. My vows and prayers
89    Yet are the king's, and till my soul forsake
90    Shall cry for blessings on him. May he live
91    Longer than I have time to tell his years;
      Ever beloved and loving may his rule be;
93    And when old time shall lead him to his end,
94    Goodness and he fill up one monument!

---

66 *look* take care   67 *build . . . graves of* erect their evil designs on the death
of   71 *make faults* commit offenses   74 *Is only . . . dying* is the only thing
bitter to him, the only death   77 *sacrifice* offering   78 *a* in   85 *envy* malice
89 *forsake* leave the body   91 *tell* count   93 *old time* old age   94 *monument*
tomb

LOVELL
   To th' waterside I must conduct your grace,
   Then give my charge up to Sir Nicholas Vaux,
   Who undertakes you to your end.               97
VAUX                          Prepare there,
   The duke is coming. See the barge be ready
   And fit it with such furniture as suits       99
   The greatness of his person.                *100*
BUCKINGHAM             Nay, Sir Nicholas,
   Let it alone; my state now will but mock me.   101
   When I came hither I was Lord High Constable
   And Duke of Buckingham; now poor Edward Bohun.
   Yet I am richer than my base accusers,
   That never knew what truth meant. I now seal it,   105
   And with that blood will make 'em one day groan for't.
   My noble father, Henry of Buckingham,
   Who first raised head against usurping Richard,   108
   Flying for succor to his servant Banister,
   Being distressed, was by that wretch betrayed,   *110*
   And without trial fell. God's peace be with him!
   Henry the Seventh succeeding, truly pitying
   My father's loss, like a most royal prince
   Restored me to my honors; and out of ruins
   Made my name once more noble. Now his son,
   Henry the Eighth, life, honor, name, and all
   That made me happy, at one stroke has taken
   For ever from the world. I had my trial,
   And must needs say a noble one; which makes me
   A little happier than my wretched father.       *120*
   Yet thus far we are one in fortunes: both
   Fell by our servants, by those men we loved most –
   A most unnatural and faithless service.
   Heaven has an end in all; yet you that hear me,   124

---

97 *undertakes* conducts  99 *furniture* equipment  101 *state* noble accoutrements  105 *seal* ratify  108 *raised head* gathered a force  124 *end* purpose

125   This from a dying man receive as certain:
      Where you are liberal of your loves and counsels
127   Be sure you be not loose; for those you make friends
      And give your hearts to, when they once perceive
129   The least rub in your fortunes, fall away
130   Like water from ye, never found again
131   But where they mean to sink ye. All good people,
      Pray for me! I must now forsake ye; the last hour
      Of my long weary life is come upon me.
      Farewell!
      And when you would say something that is sad,
      Speak how I fell. I have done, and God forgive me!
                              *Exeunt Duke and train.*

FIRST GENTLEMAN
137   O this is full of pity! Sir, it calls,
      I fear, too many curses on their heads
      That were the authors.
SECOND GENTLEMAN     If the duke be guiltless,
140   'Tis full of woe. Yet I can give you inkling
141   Of an ensuing evil, if it fall,
      Greater than this.
FIRST GENTLEMAN     Good angels keep it from us!
143   What may it be? You do not doubt my faith, sir?
SECOND GENTLEMAN
      This secret is so weighty 'twill require
      A strong faith to conceal it.
FIRST GENTLEMAN                 Let me have it.
146   I do not talk much.
SECOND GENTLEMAN  I am confident.
      You shall, sir. Did you not of late days hear
148   A buzzing of a separation
149   Between the king and Katherine?
FIRST GENTLEMAN                 Yes, but it held not;

---

125 *receive as certain* accept as truth   127 *loose* unrestrained   129 *rub* obstruction   131 *sink* ruin   137 *calls* calls down   141 *fall* occur   143 *faith* trustworthiness   146 *I am confident* I trust you   148 *buzzing* rumor   149 *held not* did not continue

For when the king once heard it, out of anger                                150
He sent command to the lord mayor straight                                   151
To stop the rumor and allay those tongues                                    152
That durst disperse it.

SECOND GENTLEMAN    But that slander, sir,
Is found a truth now; for it grows again
Fresher than e'er it was, and held for certain                               155
The king will venture at it. Either the cardinal,
Or some about him near, have out of malice
To the good queen possessed him with a scruple                               158
That will undo her. To confirm this too,
Cardinal Campeius is arrived, and lately,                                     160
As all think, for this business.

FIRST GENTLEMAN                    'Tis the cardinal;
And merely to revenge him on the emperor                                     162
For not bestowing on him at his asking
The archbishopric of Toledo, this is purposed.                               164

SECOND GENTLEMAN
I think you have hit the mark. But is't not cruel
That she should feel the smart of this? The cardinal                         166
Will have his will, and she must fall.

FIRST GENTLEMAN                              'Tis woeful.
We are too open here to argue this;                                          168
Let's think in private more.                        *Exeunt.*

※

∾ **II.2** *Enter Lord Chamberlain, reading this letter.*

[CHAMBERLAIN]    "My lord, the horses your lordship sent
for, with all the care I had, I saw well chosen, ridden,    2
and furnished. They were young and handsome and of    3

---

151 *straight* straightaway    152 *allay* restrain    155 *held* accepted    158 *possessed ... scruple* raised a doubt in his mind    162 *the emperor* Charles V (Holy Roman Emperor and nephew of Queen Katherine)    164 *purposed* intended    166 *smart* sting    168 *open* exposed in public
II.2 The royal palace    2 *ridden* broken in    3 *furnished* equipped

the best breed in the north. When they were ready to
set out for London, a man of my lord cardinal's by
6 commission and main power took 'em from me, with
this reason: his master would be served before a subject,
if not before the king; which stopped our mouths, sir."
I fear he will indeed. Well, let him have them.
10 He will have all, I think.

    *Enter to the Lord Chamberlain the Dukes of Norfolk*
    *and Suffolk.*

NORFOLK
Well met, my lord chamberlain.

CHAMBERLAIN
Good day to both your graces.

SUFFOLK
How is the king employed?

CHAMBERLAIN              I left him private,
14 Full of sad thoughts and troubles.

NORFOLK                       What's the cause?

CHAMBERLAIN
It seems the marriage with his brother's wife
Has crept too near his conscience.

SUFFOLK  *[Aside]*          No, his conscience
Has crept too near another lady.

NORFOLK                     'Tis so.
This is the cardinal's doing. The king-cardinal,
19 That blind priest, like the eldest son of Fortune,
20 Turns what he list. The king will know him one day.

SUFFOLK
Pray God he do; he'll never know himself else.

NORFOLK
How holily he works in all his business
23 And with what zeal! For, now he has cracked the league
Between us and the emperor, the queen's great nephew,
He dives into the king's soul, and there scatters

---

**6** *commission* legal writ; *main power* brute force    **14** *sad* serious    **19** *blind*
i.e., arbitrary    **23** *cracked* broken

Dangers, doubts, wringing of the conscience,                    26
Fears, and despairs, and all these for his marriage.
And out of all these, to restore the king,
He counsels a divorce, a loss of her
That like a jewel has hung twenty years                         30
. About his neck, yet never lost her luster;
Of her that loves him with that excellence                      32
That angels love good men with; even of her
That, when the greatest stroke of fortune falls,                34
Will bless the king. And is not this course pious?

CHAMBERLAIN
Heaven keep me from such counsel! 'Tis most true
These news are everywhere, every tongue speaks 'em,
And every true heart weeps for't. All that dare
Look into these affairs see this main end:                      39
The French king's sister. Heaven will one day open             40
The king's eyes that so long have slept upon                    41
This bold bad man.

SUFFOLK              And free us from his slavery.

NORFOLK
We had need pray,                                               43
And heartily, for our deliverance,                              44
Or this imperious man will work us all
From princes into pages. All men's honors
Lie like one lump before him, to be fashioned                   47
Into what pitch he please.                                      48

SUFFOLK                    For me, my lords,
I love him not, nor fear him. There's my creed:
As I am made without him, so I'll stand,                        50
If the king please. His curses and his blessings
Touch me alike; th' are breath I not believe in.
I knew him, and I know him: so I leave him

---

26 *wringing* torture   30 *jewel* gold chain (worn by men)   32 *excellence* virtuous devotion   34 *stroke* blow   39 *end* object   41 *slept upon* been closed to
43 *had need* had better   44 *heartily* wholeheartedly   47 *lump* i.e., lump of
clay   48 *pitch* level, status   50 *stand* stand firm, remain

To him that made him proud, the pope.

NORFOLK                                   Let's in,
And with some other business put the king
From these sad thoughts that work too much upon
    him.
My lord, you'll bear us company?

CHAMBERLAIN                               Excuse me.
The king has sent me otherwise. Besides,
You'll find a most unfit time to disturb him.
60      Health to your lordships!

NORFOLK                    Thanks, my good lord cham-
    berlain.    *Exit Lord Chamberlain; and the King draws*
                        *the curtain and sits reading pensively.*

SUFFOLK
61      How sad he looks. Sure he is much afflicted.

KING
Who's there, ha?

NORFOLK            Pray God he be not angry.

KING
Who's there, I say? How dare you thrust yourselves
Into my private meditations?
Who am I? ha?

NORFOLK
A gracious king that pardons all offenses
67      Malice ne'er meant. Our breach of duty this way
68      Is business of estate; in which we come
To know your royal pleasure.

KING                              Ye are too bold.
70      Go to! I'll make ye know your times of business.
71      Is this an hour for temporal affairs? ha?
        *Enter Wolsey and Campeius with a commission.*
Who's there? My good lord cardinal? O my Wolsey,
The quiet of my wounded conscience;

---

61 *sad* serious; *afflicted* troubled   67 *Malice* evil intent; *this way* in this respect   68 *estate* state   71 *temporal* worldly

Thou art a cure fit for a king. *[To Campeius]* You're wel-
come,
Most learned reverend sir, into our kingdom.
Use us and it. *[To Wolsey]* My good lord, have great care
I be not found a talker.                                                    77
WOLSEY                          Sir, you cannot.
I would your grace would give us but an hour
Of private conference.
KING   *[To Norfolk and Suffolk]*
                               We are busy: go.
NORFOLK    *[Aside to Suffolk]*
This priest has no pride in him?                                 80
SUFFOLK    *[Aside to Norfolk]*       Not to speak of.
I would not be so sick though for his place.         81
But this cannot continue.
NORFOLK    *[Aside to Suffolk]* If it do,
I'll venture one; have at him!                               83
SUFFOLK    *[Aside to Norfolk]*    I another.
                               *Exeunt Norfolk and Suffolk.*
WOLSEY
Your grace has given a precedent of wisdom
Above all princes in committing freely
Your scruple to the voice of Christendom.           86
Who can be angry now? What envy reach you?    87
The Spaniard, tied by blood and favor to her,
Must now confess, if they have any goodness,
The trial just and noble. All the clerks               90
(I mean the learned ones in Christian kingdoms)
Have their free voices. Rome, the nurse of judgment, 92
Invited by your noble self, hath sent
One general tongue unto us, this good man,       94
This just and learned priest, Cardinal Campeius,

---

77 *I . . . talker* i.e., that this not turn out to be idle talk   81 *sick . . . place*
i.e., sick with pride even to gain his position   83 *I'll . . . one* i.e., I'll be one
of those who take him on; *have at him* (a challenge, directed aside at Wolsey)
86 *voice* vote   87 *envy* malice   90 *clerks* scholars   92 *voices* votes   94 *general tongue* spokesperson for all

Whom once more I present unto your highness.

KING
And once more in mine arms I bid him welcome
98  And thank the holy conclave for their loves.
They have sent me such a man I would have wished
for.

CAMPEIUS
100  Your grace must needs deserve all strangers' loves,
You are so noble. To your highness' hand
I tender my commission, by whose virtue,
The court of Rome commanding, you, my Lord
Cardinal of York, are joined with me their servant
In the unpartial judging of this business.

KING
106  Two equal men. The queen shall be acquainted
Forthwith for what you come. Where's Gardiner?

WOLSEY
I know your majesty has always loved her
So dear in heart, not to deny her that
110  A woman of less place might ask by law –
Scholars allowed freely to argue for her.

KING
Ay, and the best she shall have; and my favor
To him that does best, God forbid else. Cardinal,
Prithee call Gardiner to me, my new secretary.
I find him a fit fellow.                    *[Exit Wolsey.]*
    *Enter [Wolsey, with] Gardiner.*

WOLSEY   *[Aside to Gardiner]*
Give me your hand. Much joy and favor to you;
You are the king's now.

GARDINER   *[Aside to Wolsey]*
                         But to be commanded
For ever by your grace, whose hand has raised me.

---

**98** *conclave* assembly of Catholic cardinals  **100** *strangers'* foreigners'  **106**
*equal* impartial  **110** *less place* lower rank

KING
  Come hither, Gardiner.
  *Walks and whispers.*
CAMPEIUS
  My Lord of York, was not one Doctor Pace                    *120*
  In this man's place before him?
WOLSEY                              Yes, he was.
CAMPEIUS
  Was he not held a learned man?
WOLSEY                              Yes, surely.
CAMPEIUS
  Believe me, there's an ill opinion spread then,
  Even of yourself, lord cardinal.
WOLSEY                              How? Of me?
CAMPEIUS
  They will not stick to say you envied him,                  *125*
  And fearing he would rise (he was so virtuous),
  Kept him a foreign man still, which so grieved him          *127*
  That he ran mad and died.
WOLSEY                              Heav'n's peace be with him!
  That's Christian care enough. For living murmurers          *129*
  There's places of rebuke. He was a fool,                    *130*
  For he would needs be virtuous. That good fellow,
  If I command him, follows my appointment;                   *132*
  I will have none so near else. Learn this, brother,         *133*
  We live not to be griped by meaner persons.                 *134*
KING
  Deliver this with modesty to th' queen.   *Exit Gardiner.*  *135*
  The most convenient place that I can think of
  For such receipt of learning is Blackfriars.                *137*
  There ye shall meet about this weighty business.

---

125 *stick* scruple   127 *Kept . . . still* i.e., constantly employed him on foreign missions   129 *murmurers* grumblers   130 *places of rebuke* correctional
institutions   132 *appointment* directions   133 *near* familiar   134 *griped*
grasped by the hand; *meaner* lesser   135 *Deliver . . . modesty* inform the
queen without making too much of it   137 *receipt . . . learning* (1) receiving
learned men, (2) hearing learned discourses

139 My Wolsey, see it furnished. O my lord,
140 Would it not grieve an able man to leave
  So sweet a bedfellow? But conscience, conscience!
  O 'tis a tender place, and I must leave her.  *Exeunt.*

*

∾ **II.3** *Enter Anne Bullen and an Old Lady.*

ANNE
1 Not for that neither; here's the pang that pinches:
  His highness having lived so long with her, and she
  So good a lady that no tongue could ever
  Pronounce dishonor of her – by my life,
  She never knew harmdoing – O, now after
6 So many courses of the sun enthronèd,
7 Still growing in a majesty and pomp, the which
  To leave a thousandfold more bitter than
9 'Tis sweet at first t' acquire – after this process
10 To give her the avaunt, it is a pity
11 Would move a monster.

OLD LADY      Hearts of most hard temper
  Melt and lament for her.

ANNE        O God's will, much better
13 She ne'er had known pomp. Though't be temporal,
14 Yet if that quarrel, fortune, do divorce
15 It from the bearer, 'tis a sufferance panging
  As soul and body's severing.

OLD LADY     Alas, poor lady,
17 She's a stranger now again.

ANNE      So much the more
  Must pity drop upon her. Verily

---

**139** *furnished* duly prepared
 **II.3** The queen's apartments **1** *pinches* hurts **6** *courses . . . enthronèd*
years **7–8** *the which / To leave* to leave which **9** *process* proceeding **10**
*avaunt* dismissal **11** *temper* disposition **13** *temporal* earthly, transient **14**
*quarrel* troublemaker **15** *sufferance panging* painful suffering **17** *stranger*
foreigner

I swear 'tis better to be lowly born
And range with humble livers in content                      20
Than to be perked up in a glist'ring grief                  21
And wear a golden sorrow.
OLD LADY                        Our content
  Is our best having.                                       23
ANNE                    By my troth and maidenhead,
  I would not be a queen.                                   24
OLD LADY                    Beshrew me, I would,
  And venture maidenhead for't; and so would you,
  For all this spice of your hypocrisy.                     26
  You that have so fair parts of women on you              27
  Have, too, a woman's heart, which ever yet
  Affected eminence, wealth, sovereignty;                  29
  Which, to say sooth, are blessings; and which gifts      30
  (Saving your mincing) the capacity                       31
  Of your soft cheveril conscience would receive,          32
  If you might please to stretch it.                       33
ANNE                            Nay, good troth.
OLD LADY
  Yes troth, and troth. You would not be a queen?
ANNE
  No, not for all the riches under heaven.
OLD LADY
  'Tis strange. A threepence bowed would hire me,          36
  Old as I am, to queen it. But I pray you,                37
  What think you of a duchess? Have you limbs
  To bear that load of title?
ANNE                        No, in truth.

---

20 *range . . . livers* rank with humble people   21 *perked up in* uplifted into
23 *having* possession   24 *queen* (Anne's first use of this term sets up a series
of puns on "quean" as prostitute in the ensuing dialogue); *Beshrew me* woe
befall me   26 *spice* dash   27 *fair parts* attractive qualities   29 *Affected* desired   30 *to say sooth* to tell the truth   31 *mincing* hypocritical affectation
32 *cheveril* i.e., like soft, pliable leather   33, 34 *troth* faith (but punning on
"trot," old hag)   36 *bowed* bent, therefore worthless (with pun on "bawd")
37 *queen* (pun on "quean")

OLD LADY
40    Then you are weakly made. Pluck off a little;
41    I would not be a young count in your way
42    For more than blushing comes to. If your back
43    Cannot vouchsafe this burden, 'tis too weak
       Ever to get a boy.

ANNE           How you do talk!
       I swear again, I would not be a queen
46    For all the world.

OLD LADY        In faith, for little England
47    You'd venture an emballing. I myself
48    Would for Carnarvonshire, although there longed
       No more to th' crown but that. Lo, who comes here?
       *Enter Lord Chamberlain.*

CHAMBERLAIN
50    Good morrow, ladies. What were't worth to know
       The secret of your conference?

ANNE               My good lord,
52    Not your demand; it values not your asking.
       Our mistress' sorrows we were pitying.

CHAMBERLAIN
       It was a gentle business and becoming
       The action of good women. There is hope
       All will be well.

ANNE           Now I pray God, amen.

CHAMBERLAIN
       You bear a gentle mind, and heav'nly blessings
       Follow such creatures. That you may, fair lady,
       Perceive I speak sincerely, and high note's

---

**40** *Pluck off* (1) come down a level, (2) remove the fancy dress  **41** *count* (an aristocratic rank, with possible pun on "cunt")  **42** *For . . . comes to* i.e., with (no) more fuss than a blush (i.e., she would yield herself quite happily)  **43** *vouchsafe* tolerate (i.e., bearing the weight of a man)  **46** *little England* (a term sometimes applied to Pembrokeshire, but also applicable to England as a whole)  **47** *an emballing* (1) being invested with the orb of royalty, (2) having sex (being balled)  **48** *Carnarvonshire* a barren county in Wales; *longed* belonged  **52** *Not . . . demand* don't ask

Ta'en of your many virtues, the king's majesty                    60
Commends his good opinion of you, and                             61
Does purpose honor to you no less flowing
Than Marchioness of Pembroke; to which title
A thousand pound a year, annual support,
Out of his grace he adds.
ANNE                              I do not know
What kind of my obedience I should tender.
More than my all is nothing; nor my prayers                       67
Are not words duly hallowed, nor my wishes
More worth than empty vanities; yet prayers and
    wishes
Are all I can return. Beseech your lordship,                      70
Vouchsafe to speak my thanks and my obedience,                    71
As from a blushing handmaid, to his highness,
Whose health and royalty I pray for.
CHAMBERLAIN                              Lady,
I shall not fail t' approve the fair conceit                      74
The king hath of you. *[Aside]* I have perused her well.
Beauty and honor in her are so mingled
That they have caught the king; and who knows yet
But from this lady may proceed a gem
To lighten all this isle. – I'll to the king                      79
And say I spoke with you.                                         80
ANNE                              My honored lord.
                              *Exit Lord Chamberlain.*

OLD LADY
Why, this it is! See, see,                                        81
I have been begging sixteen years in court
(Am yet a courtier beggarly) nor could                           83
Come pat betwixt too early and too late                          84
For any suit of pounds; and you (O fate!),                       85

---

61 *Commends . . . you* sends his compliments  67–68 *nor . . . not* (double
negative for emphasis)  71 *Vouchsafe* be so kind as  74 *fair conceit* good
opinion  79 *lighten* light up  81 *this it is* this is how it goes  83 *beggarly*
poor  84 *Come pat* hit the right moment  85 *suit of pounds* petition for
money

A very fresh fish here – fie, fie, fie upon
87    This compelled fortune! – have your mouth filled up
Before you open it.

ANNE                              This is strange to me.

OLD LADY
89    How tastes it? Is it bitter? Forty pence, no.
90    There was a lady once ('tis an old story)
That would not be a queen, that would she not,
92    For all the mud in Egypt. Have you heard it?

ANNE
93    Come, you are pleasant.

OLD LADY                         With your theme I could
94    O'ermount the lark. The Marchioness of Pembroke?
A thousand pounds a year, for pure respect?
No other obligation? By my life,
97    That promises more thousands! Honor's train
Is longer than his foreskirt. By this time
I know your back will bear a duchess. Say,
100   Are you not stronger than you were?

ANNE                                    Good lady,
101   Make yourself mirth with your particular fancy
And leave me out on't. Would I had no being
103   If this salute my blood a jot! It faints me
To think what follows.
The queen is comfortless, and we forgetful
106   In our long absence. Pray do not deliver
What here y' have heard to her.

OLD LADY                        What do you think me?
                                            *Exeunt.*

                          *

---

87 *compelled* i.e., thrust upon her   89 *Forty pence, no* i.e., I'll bet you forty
pence that it doesn't   92 *mud in Egypt* i.e., the wealth of Egypt, based on the
fertile Nile valley   93 *pleasant* humorous   94 *O'ermount* rise higher than
101 *particular* private   103 *salute . . . jot* i.e., excites me in the least; *faints
me* makes me feel faint   106 *deliver* make known

∾ **II.4**  *Trumpets, sennet, and cornets.*
*Enter two Vergers, with short silver wands; next them,*
*two Scribes, in the habit of doctors; after them, the*
*[Arch]bishop of Canterbury alone; after him, the*
*Bishops of Lincoln, Ely, Rochester, and Saint Asaph;*
*next them, with some small distance, follows a*
*Gentleman bearing the purse, with the great seal and a*
*cardinal's hat; then two Priests, bearing each a silver*
*cross; then [Griffith,] a Gentleman Usher, bareheaded,*
*accompanied with a Sergeant at Arms bearing a silver*
*mace; then two Gentlemen bearing two great silver*
*pillars; after them, side by side, the two Cardinals, two*
*Noblemen with the sword and mace. The King takes*
*place under the cloth of state; the two Cardinals sit*
*under him as Judges. The Queen takes place some*
*distance from the King. The Bishops place themselves*
*on each side the court, in manner of a consistory;*
*below them, the Scribes. The Lords sit next the Bishops.*
*The rest of the Attendants stand in convenient order*
*about the stage.*

WOLSEY
　Whilst our commission from Rome is read,
　Let silence be commanded.
KING　　　　　　　　　　　　What's the need?
　It hath already publicly been read,
　And on all sides th' authority allowed.　　　　　　4
　You may then spare that time.
WOLSEY　　　　　　　　　　Be't so. Proceed.

---

II.4 The court at Blackfriars **s.d.** *sennet* trumpet fanfare; *cornets* horns; *Vergers* officials who carry the symbols of office before dignitaries of the church or university; *Scribes* secretaries; *the habit of doctors* doctoral gowns and hoods; *silver pillars* (Wolsey's personal emblem, in addition to the silver mace to which he is entitled as a cardinal); *takes place* seats himself; *consistory* council chamber   4 *allowed* acknowledged

SCRIBE
  Say, "Henry King of England, come into the court."
CRIER
  Henry King of England, etc.
KING
  Here.
SCRIBE
  Say, "Katherine Queen of England, come into the
  court."
CRIER
10  Katherine Queen of England, etc.
  *The Queen makes no answer, rises out of her chair,*
  *goes about the court, comes to the King, and kneels at*
  *his feet; then speaks.*
[KATHERINE]
  Sir, I desire you do me right and justice,
  And to bestow your pity on me; for
13  I am a most poor woman and a stranger,
  Born out of your dominions: having here
15  No judge indifferent, nor no more assurance
16  Of equal friendship and proceeding. Alas, sir,
  In what have I offended you? What cause
  Hath my behavior given to your displeasure
19  That thus you should proceed to put me off
20  And take your good grace from me? Heaven witness,
  I have been to you a true and humble wife,
22  At all times to your will conformable,
  Ever in fear to kindle your dislike,
  Yea, subject to your countenance, glad or sorry
  As I saw it inclined. When was the hour
  I ever contradicted your desire
  Or made it not mine too? Or which of your friends
  Have I not strove to love, although I knew
  He were mine enemy? What friend of mine

---

13 *stranger* foreigner  15 *indifferent* impartial  16 *equal* fair  19 *put me off*
discard me  20 *good grace* favor and person  22 *conformable* conforming

That had to him derived your anger, did I                    30
Continue in my liking? Nay, gave notice
He was from thence discharged? Sir, call to mind
That I have been your wife in this obedience
Upward of twenty years, and have been blessed
With many children by you. If in the course
And process of this time you can report,
And prove it too, against mine honor aught,
My bond to wedlock, or my love and duty
Against your sacred person, in God's name                    39
Turn me away, and let the foul'st contempt                   40
Shut door upon me, and so give me up
To the sharp'st kind of justice. Please you, sir,
The king your father was reputed for
A prince most prudent, of an excellent
And unmatched wit and judgment. Ferdinand,                   45
My father, King of Spain, was reckoned one                   46
The wisest prince that there had reigned by many
A year before. It is not to be questioned
That they had gathered a wise council to them
Of every realm, that did debate this business,              50
Who deemed our marriage lawful. Wherefore I humbly
Beseech you, sir, to spare me till I may
Be by my friends in Spain advised, whose counsel
I will implore. If not, i' th' name of God,
Your pleasure be fulfilled!
WOLSEY                      You have here, lady
(And of your choice), these reverend fathers, men
Of singular integrity and learning,
Yea, the elect o' th' land, who are assembled
To plead your cause. It shall be therefore bootless         59
That longer you desire the court, as well                    60
For your own quiet as to rectify

---

30 *derived* attracted   39 *Against* toward   45 *unmatched* incomparable; *wit*
wisdom   46 *one* one of   59 *bootless* fruitless   60 *desire* i.e., to delay the
business

What is unsettled in the king.

CAMPEIUS                              His grace
Hath spoken well and justly. Therefore, madam,
It's fit this royal session do proceed
And that without delay their arguments
Be now produced and heard.

KATHERINE                              Lord cardinal,
To you I speak.

WOLSEY              Your pleasure, madam.

KATHERINE                                   Sir,
I am about to weep; but, thinking that
69    We are a queen (or long have dreamed so), certain
70    The daughter of a king, my drops of tears
I'll turn to sparks of fire.

WOLSEY                        Be patient yet.

KATHERINE
I will, when you are humble; nay before,
Or God will punish me. I do believe
74    (Induced by potent circumstances) that
75    You are mine enemy, and make my challenge,
You shall not be my judge. For it is you
77    Have blown this coal betwixt my lord and me,
Which God's dew quench! Therefore I say again
79    I utterly abhor, yea, from my soul
80    Refuse you for my judge, whom yet once more
I hold my most malicious foe and think not
82    At all a friend to truth.

WOLSEY                        I do profess
You speak not like yourself, who ever yet
84    Have stood to charity and displayed th' effects
Of disposition gentle, and of wisdom
O'ertopping woman's pow'r. Madam, you do me
    wrong.

---

69 *certain* certainly  74 *Induced* persuaded  75 *challenge* legal objection
77 *blown this coal* i.e., created this strife  79 *abhor* protest, reject  82 *profess*
affirm  84 *stood to* upheld

I have no spleen against you, nor injustice                              87
For you or any. How far I have proceeded,
Or how far further shall, is warranted
By a commission from the consistory,                                     90
Yea, the whole consistory of Rome. You charge me
That I have blown this coal: I do deny it.
The king is present. If it be known to him
That I gainsay my deed, how may he wound,                                94
And worthily, my falsehood, yea, as much                                 95
As you have done my truth. If he know
That I am free of your report, he knows                                  97
I am not of your wrong. Therefore in him                                 98
It lies to cure me, and the cure is to
Remove these thoughts from you; the which before                        *100*
His highness shall speak in, I do beseech                                101
You, gracious madam, to unthink your speaking
And to say so no more.
KATHERINE                    My lord, my lord,
I am a simple woman, much too weak
T' oppose your cunning. You're meek and humble-
    mouthed;
You sign your place and calling, in full seeming,                        106
With meekness and humility, but your heart
Is crammed with arrogancy, spleen, and pride.                            108
You have, by fortune and his highness' favors,
Gone slightly o'er low steps, and now are mounted                        110
Where pow'rs are your retainers, and your words      ·                   111
(Domestics to you) serve your will as't please
Yourself pronounce their office. I must tell you
You tender more your person's honor than                                 114

---

87 *spleen* anger   90 *consistory* assembly of cardinals   94 *gainsay my deed*
deny what I have done   95 *worthily* deservedly   97 *free of your report* innocent of your charge   98 *I . . . wrong* i.e., I have done nothing to injure you
101 *in* in reference to   106 *sign your place* signify your office   108 *spleen*
anger, malice   110 *slightly* easily   111 *pow'rs* powerful people   111–13
*your words . . . office* i.e., your words are immediately acted upon, as if they
were your servants   114 *tender* cherish

Your high profession spiritual; that again
I do refuse you for my judge and here,
Before you all, appeal unto the pope,
To bring my whole cause 'fore his holiness
119   And to be judged by him.
      *She curtsies to the King and offers to depart.*

CAMPEIUS                        The queen is obstinate,
120   Stubborn to justice, apt to accuse it, and
      Disdainful to be tried by't. 'Tis not well.
      She's going away.

KING
      Call her again.

CRIER
      Katherine Queen of England, come into the court.

GRIFFITH
      Madam, you are called back.

KATHERINE
126   What need you note it? Pray you keep your way;
      When you are called, return. Now the Lord help,
      They vex me past my patience. Pray you pass on.
      I will not tarry; no, nor ever more
130   Upon this business my appearance make
      In any of their courts. *Exeunt Queen and her Attendants.*

KING                        Go thy ways, Kate.
      That man i' th' world who shall report he has
      A better wife, let him in nought be trusted
      For speaking false in that. Thou art alone
135   (If thy rare qualities, sweet gentleness,
136   Thy meekness saintlike, wifelike government,
137   Obeying in commanding, and thy parts
138   Sovereign and pious else, could speak thee out)
      The queen of earthly queens. She's noble born,
140   And like her true nobility she has

---

119 s.d. *offers* ventures   120 *Stubborn to* resistant to   126 *keep your way*
keep on your way   135 *rare* excelling   136 *government* self-control   137
*parts* qualities   138 *speak thee out* accurately describe you

Carried herself towards me.                                       141
WOLSEY                          Most gracious sir,
  In humblest manner I require your highness             142
  That it shall please you to declare in hearing
  Of all these ears (for where I am robbed and bound
  There must I be unloosed, although not there
  At once and fully satisfied) whether ever I             146
  Did broach this business to your highness, or
  Laid any scruple in your way which might
  Induce you to the question on't; or ever                149
  Have to you, but with thanks to God for such            *150*
  A royal lady, spake one the least word that might       151
  Be to the prejudice of her present state                152
  Or touch of her good person.                            153
KING                             My lord cardinal,
  I do excuse you; yea, upon mine honor,                  154
  I free you from't. You are not to be taught
  That you have many enemies that know not
  Why they are so, but like to village curs
  Bark when their fellows do. By some of these
  The queen is put in anger. You're excused.
  But will you be more justified? You ever                 *160*
  Have wished the sleeping of this business; never desired
  It to be stirred, but oft have hindered, oft
  The passages made toward it. On my honor,               163
  I speak my good lord card'nal to this point,
  And thus far clear him. Now what moved me to't,
  I will be bold with time and your attention:
  Then mark th' inducement. Thus it came; give heed  167
    to't:
  My conscience first received a tenderness,
  Scruple and prick, on certain speeches uttered

---

141 *Carried* conducted   142 *require* request   146 *satisfied* given satisfaction
149 *to the question on't* i.e., to take up the issue   151 *one the least* the least
152 *prejudice* detriment   153 *touch* sullying   154 *excuse* exculpate   163
*passages* proceedings   167 *inducement* instigation

170  By th' Bishop of Bayonne, then French ambassador,
     Who had been hither sent on the debating
     A marriage 'twixt the Duke of Orleans and
     Our daughter Mary. I' th' progress of this business,
174  Ere a determinate resolution, he
175  (I mean the bishop) did require a respite,
176  Wherein he might the king his lord advertise
     Whether our daughter were legitimate,
     Respecting this our marriage with the dowager,
179  Sometimes our brother's wife. This respite shook
180  The bosom of my conscience, entered me,
181  Yea, with a spitting power, and made to tremble
     The region of my breast, which forced such way
183  That many mazed considerings did throng
     And pressed in with this caution. First, methought
185  I stood not in the smile of heaven, who had
     Commanded nature that my lady's womb,
     If it conceived a male child by me, should
188  Do no more offices of life to't than
     The grave does to th' dead; for her male issue
190  Or died where they were made or shortly after
191  This world had aired them. Hence I took a thought
     This was a judgment on me, that my kingdom
     (Well worthy the best heir o' th' world) should not
     Be gladded in't by me. Then follows that
     I weighed the danger which my realms stood in
196  By this my issue's fail, and that gave to me
197  Many a groaning throe. Thus hulling in
     The wild sea of my conscience, I did steer

---

174 *determinate resolution* final settlement  175 *require a respite* request a
delay  176 *advertise* inform  179 *Sometimes* formerly (Katherine had previously been married to Henry's elder brother Arthur, the heir apparent, who
had died, as a result of which Henry became king and married Katherine)
181 *spitting* piercing  183 *mazed* perplexed  185 *smile* good graces  188
*offices* services  190 *Or... or* either... or  191 *aired them* given them
breath  196 *issue's fail* failure to produce (male) heirs  197 *throe* fit of an-
guish; *hulling* adrift

Toward this remedy whereupon we are
Now present here together. That's to say                    *200*
I mean to rectify my conscience, which                     201
I then did feel full sick, and yet not well,              202
By all the reverend fathers of the land
And doctors learned. First I began in private             204
With you, my Lord of Lincoln. You remember
How under my oppression I did reek                        206
When I first moved you.                                   207

LINCOLN                          Very well, my liege.

KING
I have spoke long. Be pleased yourself to say
How far you satisfied me.

LINCOLN                          So please your highness,
The question did at first so stagger me,                  *210*
Bearing a state of mighty moment in't                     211
And consequence of dread, that I committed                212
The daring'st counsel which I had to doubt
And did entreat your highness to this course
Which you are running here.

KING                               I then moved you,
My Lord of Canterbury, and got your leave
To make this present summons. Unsolicited
I left no reverend person in this court,
But by particular consent proceeded
Under your hands and seals. Therefore go on,             220
For no dislike i' th' world against the person
Of the good queen, but the sharp thorny points
Of my allegèd reasons, drives this forward.              223
Prove but our marriage lawful, by my life
And kingly dignity, we are contented

---

201 *rectify* clear, set right   202 *yet* still   204 *doctors* lawyers, scholars   **206**
*oppression* distress; *reek* sweat   207 *moved* appealed to   211 *Bearing . . . mo-*
*ment* concerning a situation of great importance   212 *consequence of dread*
fearful outcome   212–13 *committed . . . to doubt* i.e., gave, although doubt-
fully, my boldest advice   220 *Under . . . seals* with your written and signed
consent   223 *allegèd* already stated

226     To wear our mortal state to come with her,
       Katherine our queen, before the primest creature
228     That's paragoned o' th' world.
CAMPEIUS                 So please your highness,
       The queen being absent, 'tis a needful fitness
230     That we adjourn this court till further day.
231     Meanwhile must be an earnest motion
       Made to the queen to call back her appeal
       She intends unto his holiness.
KING   *[Aside]*             I may perceive
       These cardinals trifle with me. I abhor
       This dilatory sloth and tricks of Rome.
       My learned and well-belovèd servant Cranmer,
       Prithee return. With thy approach I know
       My comfort comes along. – Break up the court;
       I say set on.         *Exeunt, in manner as they entered.*

                    *

∾ **III.1**  *Enter the Queen and her Women, as at work.*

KATHERINE
    Take thy lute, wench, my soul grows sad with troubles;
2     Sing, and disperse 'em if thou canst. Leave working.
                  *Song.*
         Orpheus with his lute made trees,
         And the mountain tops that freeze,
            Bow themselves when he did sing.
         To his music plants and flowers
7          Ever sprung, as sun and showers
            There had made a lasting spring.

         Every thing that heard him play,
10         Even the billows of the sea,

---

226 *mortal state* i.e., garb and appurtenances of kingship  228 *paragoned*
held up as model of excellence  230 *further day* a future date  231 *motion*
plea
    III.1 The queen's apartments  2 *Leave* cease  7 *as* as if

> Hung their heads, and then lay by.                11
> In sweet music is such art,
> Killing care and grief of heart
> Fall asleep, or hearing die.

*Enter a Gentleman.*

KATHERINE
How now?

GENTLEMAN
An't please your grace, the two great cardinals        16
Wait in the presence.                                  17

KATHERINE                          Would they speak with me?

GENTLEMAN
They willed me say so, madam.                          18

KATHERINE                          Pray their graces
To come near.                        *[Exit Gentleman.]*
                    What can be their business
With me, a poor weak woman, fall'n from favor?         20
I do not like their coming. Now I think on't,
They should be good men, their affairs as righteous,   22
But all hoods make not monks.

*Enter the two Cardinals, Wolsey and Campeius.*

WOLSEY                             Peace to your highness.

KATHERINE
Your graces find me here part of a housewife
(I would be all) against the worst may happen.          25
What are your pleasures with me, reverend lords?

WOLSEY
May it please you, noble madam, to withdraw
Into your private chamber, we shall give you
The full cause of our coming.

KATHERINE                          Speak it here.
There's nothing I have done yet, o' my conscience,      30
Deserves a corner. Would all other women               31

---

11 *lay by* rested   16 *An't* if it   17 *presence* presence chamber   18 *willed* requested   22 *affairs* business   25 *would be* wish I were; *against* in preparation for   31 *a corner* i.e., secrecy

32     Could speak this with as free a soul as I do!
    My lords, I care not (so much I am happy
34     Above a number) if my actions
    Were tried by ev'ry tongue, ev'ry eye saw 'em,
36     Envy and base opinion set against 'em,
37     I know my life so even. If your business
38     Seek me out, and that way I am wife in,
    Out with it boldly: truth loves open dealing.
40 WOLSEY    *Tanta est erga te mentis integritas, regina serenis-*
    *sima* –
    KATHERINE
    O, good my lord, no Latin!
43     I am not such a truant since my coming
    As not to know the language I have lived in.
45     A strange tongue makes my cause more strange, suspi-
    cious.
    Pray speak in English. Here are some will thank you,
    If you speak truth, for their poor mistress' sake.
    Believe me, she has had much wrong. Lord cardinal,
49     The willing'st sin I ever yet committed
50     May be absolved in English.
    WOLSEY                  Noble lady,
    I am sorry my integrity should breed
    (And service to his majesty and you)
53     So deep suspicion where all faith was meant.
54     We come not by the way of accusation
    To taint that honor every good tongue blesses,
56     Nor to betray you any way to sorrow –
    You have too much, good lady – but to know
    How you stand minded in the weighty difference

---

32 *free* innocent   34 *a number* many   36 *Envy* malice; *opinion* gossip   37 *even* constant (in its uprightness)   38 *that way I am wife in* i.e., pertaining to my situation as a wife   40–41 *Tanta . . . serenissima* such is the honesty of my mind toward you, O most serene queen   43 *truant* idler   45 *strange . . . strange* foreign . . . unfamiliar   49 *willing'st* most deliberate   53 *faith* loyalty   54 *by the way . . . accusation* in order to accuse you   56 *any way* in any manner

Between the king and you, and to deliver                           59
(Like free and honest men) our just opinions                      60
And comforts to your cause.

CAMPEIUS                          Most honored madam,
My Lord of York, out of his noble nature,
Zeal and obedience he still bore your grace,                       63
Forgetting (like a good man) your late censure
Both of his truth and him (which was too far),                     65
Offers, as I do, in a sign of peace,                              66
His service and his counsel.

KATHERINE    *[Aside]*          To betray me. –
My lords, I thank you both for your good wills,
Ye speak like honest men (pray God ye prove so).
But how to make ye suddenly an answer                             70
In such a point of weight, so near mine honor                     71
(More near my life, I fear), with my weak wit,                    72
And to such men of gravity and learning,
In truth I know not. I was set at work                            74
Among my maids, full little (God knows) looking
Either for such men or such business.
For her sake that I have been – for I feel
The last fit of my greatness – good your graces,                  78
Let me have time and counsel for my cause.
Alas, I am a woman friendless, hopeless.                           80

WOLSEY
Madam, you wrong the king's love with these fears.
Your hopes and friends are infinite.

KATHERINE                                  In England
But little for my profit. Can you think, lords,
That any Englishman dare give me counsel?
Or be a known friend 'gainst his highness' pleasure
(Though he be grown so desperate to be honest)                    86

---

59 *deliver* convey  60 *honest* honorable  63 *still* always  65 *was* went  66
*in a sign* as a token  70 *suddenly* on the spur of the moment  71 *near* inti-
mately affecting  72 *wit* understanding  74 *set* seated  78 *last fit* death
spasm  86 *so desperate . . . honest* so reckless as to tell the truth

And live a subject? Nay forsooth, my friends,
88      They that must weigh out my afflictions,
        They that my trust must grow to, live not here.
90      They are (as all my other comforts) far hence
        In mine own country, lords.
CAMPEIUS                    I would your grace
        Would leave your griefs and take my counsel.
KATHERINE                                How, sir?
CAMPEIUS
        Put your main cause into the king's protection,
        He's loving and most gracious. 'Twill be much
        Both for your honor better and your cause;
        For if the trial of the law o'ertake ye,
97      You'll part away disgraced.
WOLSEY                      He tells you rightly.
KATHERINE
        Ye tell me what ye wish for both – my ruin.
        Is this your Christian counsel? Out upon ye!
100     Heaven is above all yet; there sits a judge
101     That no king can corrupt.
CAMPEIUS                    Your rage mistakes us.
KATHERINE
        The more shame for ye! Holy men I thought ye,
103     Upon my soul, two reverend cardinal virtues;
        But cardinal sins and hollow hearts I fear ye.
        Mend 'em for shame, my lords! Is this your comfort?
106     The cordial that ye bring a wretched lady?
107     A woman lost among ye, laughed at, scorned?
        I will not wish ye half my miseries,
        I have more charity. But say I warned ye.
110     Take heed, for heaven's sake take heed, lest at once
        The burden of my sorrows fall upon ye.

---

**88** *weigh out* (1) justly measure (?), (2) help to carry the weight of   **97** *part away* leave   **101** *mistakes* misconstrues   **103** *two reverend cardinal virtues* i.e., two embodiments of the cardinal virtues faith, hope, and charity (punning on *cardinal*, as in the following line)   **106** *cordial* restorative   **107** *lost* brought to ruin   **110** *at once* all at once

WOLSEY

   Madam, this is a mere distraction.          112

   You turn the good we offer into envy.       113

KATHERINE

   Ye turn me into nothing. Woe upon ye

   And all such false professors! Would you have me   115

   (If you have any justice, any pity,

   If ye be anything but churchmen's habits)      117

   Put my sick cause into his hands that hates me?

   Alas, has banished me his bed already,       119

   His love, too long ago. I am old, my lords,     120

   And all the fellowship I hold now with him

   Is only my obedience. What can happen

   To me above this wretchedness? All your studies   123

   Make me accursed like this.          124

CAMPEIUS             Your fears are worse.

KATHERINE

   Have I lived thus long (let me speak myself,

   Since virtue finds no friends) a wife, a true one?

   A woman (I dare say without vainglory)

   Never yet branded with suspicion?

   Have I with all my full affections        129

   Still met the king? Loved him next heav'n? Obeyed him?   130

   Been (out of fondness) superstitious to him?   131

   Almost forgot my prayers to content him?

   And am I thus rewarded? 'Tis not well, lords.

   Bring me a constant woman to her husband,    134

   One that ne'er dreamed a joy beyond his pleasure,

   And to that woman (when she has done most)

   Yet will I add an honor – a great patience.

WOLSEY

   Madam, you wander from the good we aim at.

---

112 *distraction* frenzy   113 *envy* malice   115 *professors* those who profess to do, or be, good   117 *habits* outer garments   119 *has* he has   123 *studies* efforts   124 *accursed* afflicted, as if under a curse   129 *affections* love   130 *Still* always   131 *superstitious* excessively devoted   134 *constant woman to* woman constant to

KATHERINE
    My lord, I dare not make myself so guilty
140    To give up willingly that noble title
    Your master wed me to. Nothing but death
    Shall e'er divorce my dignities.
WOLSEY                      Pray hear me.
KATHERINE
    Would I had never trod this English earth
    Or felt the flatteries that grow upon it!
    Ye have angels' faces, but heaven knows your hearts.
    What will become of me now, wretched lady?
    I am the most unhappy woman living.
        *[To her Women]*
    Alas, poor wenches, where are now your fortunes?
    Shipwracked upon a kingdom where no pity,
150    No friends, no hope, no kindred weep for me,
    Almost no grave allowed me. Like the lily
    That once was mistress of the field and flourished,
    I'll hang my head and perish.
WOLSEY                  If your grace
154    Could but be brought to know our ends are honest,
    You'd feel more comfort. Why should we, good lady,
156    Upon what cause, wrong you? Alas, our places,
    The way of our profession is against it.
    We are to cure such sorrows, not to sow 'em.
    For goodness' sake, consider what you do,
160    How you may hurt yourself, ay, utterly
161    Grow from the king's acquaintance by this carriage.
    The hearts of princes kiss obedience,
    So much they love it; but to stubborn spirits
    They swell and grow as terrible as storms.
165    I know you have a gentle, noble temper,
    A soul as even as a calm. Pray think us
    Those we profess, peacemakers, friends, and servants.

---

154 *honest* honorable    156 *places* (religious) offices    161 *Grow from* become
estranged from; *carriage* behavior    165 *temper* disposition

CAMPEIUS
   Madam, you'll find it so. You wrong your virtues
   With these weak women's fears. A noble spirit,
   As yours was put into you, ever casts             170
   Such doubts as false coin from it. The king loves you:
   Beware you lose it not. For us, if you please
   To trust us in your business, we are ready
   To use our utmost studies in your service.        174
KATHERINE
   Do what ye will, my lords, and pray forgive me,
   If I have used myself unmannerly.             176
   You know I am a woman, lacking wit           177
   To make a seemly answer to such persons.
   Pray do my service to his majesty,            179
   He has my heart yet, and shall have my prayers    *180*
   While I shall have my life. Come, reverend fathers,
   Bestow your counsels on me. She now begs
   That little thought, when she set footing here,
   She should have bought her dignities so dear.   *Exeunt.*

*

  ◦~ **III.2** *Enter the Duke of Norfolk, Duke of Suffolk,*
    *Lord Surrey, and Lord Chamberlain.*

NORFOLK
   If you will now unite in your complaints
   And force them with a constancy, the cardinal    2
   Cannot stand under them. If you omit        3
   The offer of this time, I cannot promise
   But that you shall sustain more new disgraces
   With these you bear already.
SURREY                    I am joyful

---

170 *As . . . put into* i.e., such as you were endowed with   174 *studies* efforts
176 *used myself* behaved   177 *wit* (masculine) understanding   179 *do my
service* pay my respects
    III.2 The king's apartments   2 *force . . . constancy* press them home with
persistence   3 *stand under* withstand; *omit* neglect

          To meet the least occasion that may give me
8         Remembrance of my father-in-law, the duke,
          To be revenged on him.
SUFFOLK                          Which of the peers
10        Have uncontemned gone by him, or at least
          Strangely neglected? When did he regard
          The stamp of nobleness in any person
13        Out of himself?
CHAMBERLAIN      My lords, you speak your pleasures.
          What he deserves of you and me I know.
          What we can do to him (though now the time
16        Gives way to us) I much fear. If you cannot
17        Bar his access to th' king, never attempt
          Anything on him; for he hath a witchcraft
          Over the king in's tongue.
NORFOLK                          O fear him not,
20        His spell in that is out. The king hath found
          Matter against him that for ever mars
22        The honey of his language. No, he's settled
23        (Not to come off) in his displeasure.
SURREY                                    Sir,
          I should be glad to hear such news as this
          Once every hour.
NORFOLK            Believe it, this is true.
26        In the divorce his contrary proceedings
27        Are all unfolded; wherein he appears
          As I would wish mine enemy.
SURREY                          How came
29        His practices to light?
SUFFOLK              Most strangely.
SURREY                                O how? How?

---

8 *the duke* i.e., Buckingham   10 *uncontemned* without being despised   13
*Out of* apart from   16 *Gives way to* favors   17–18 *attempt / Anything* make
any attack   20 *His spell . . . out* i.e., his magical power of persuasion is ex-
hausted   22 *settled* fixed   23 *his* i.e., the king's   26 *contrary* contradictory
27 *unfolded* revealed   29 *practices* intrigues

SUFFOLK

    The cardinal's letters to the pope miscarried        30

    And came to th' eye o' th' king, wherein was read

    How that the cardinal did entreat his holiness

    To stay the judgment o' th' divorce; for if

    It did take place, "I do," quoth he, "perceive

    My king is tangled in affection to

    A creature of the queen's, Lady Anne Bullen."        36

SURREY

    Has the king this?

SUFFOLK               Believe it.

SURREY                    Will this work?

CHAMBERLAIN

    The king in this perceives him, how he coasts        38

    And hedges his own way. But in this point        39

    All his tricks founder and he brings his physic        40

    After his patient's death: the king already

    Hath married the fair lady.

SURREY                 Would he had!

SUFFOLK

    May you be happy in your wish, my lord,

    For I profess you have it.               44

SURREY             Now all my joy

    Trace the conjunction!               45

SUFFOLK           My amen to't!

NORFOLK               All men's!

SUFFOLK

    There's order given for her coronation.

    Marry this is yet but young, and may be left        47

    To some ears unrecounted. But, my lords,

    She is a gallant creature and complete        49

    In mind and feature. I persuade me, from her     50

---

30 *miscarried* went astray   36 *creature* minion, agent   38 *coasts* maneuvers circuitously   39 *hedges . . . way* dodges around for his own ends   40 *founder* sink, come to nought; *physic* medicine   44 *profess* declare   45 *Trace* follow, attend upon; *conjunction* union, marriage   47 *Marry* to be sure ("by Mary"); *young* new   49 *gallant* splendid; *complete* perfect

Will fall some blessing to this land, which shall
52    In it be memorized.

SURREY                    But will the king
53    Digest this letter of the cardinal's?
      The Lord forbid!

NORFOLK              Marry amen.

SUFFOLK                          No, no;
      There be more wasps that buzz about his nose
      Will make this sting the sooner. Cardinal Campeius
      Is stol'n away to Rome, hath ta'en no leave,
      Has left the cause o' th' king unhandled, and
59    Is posted as the agent of our cardinal
60    To second all his plot. I do assure you
61    The king cried "Ha" at this.

CHAMBERLAIN                    Now God incense him
      And let him cry "Ha" louder!

NORFOLK                        But, my lord,
      When returns Cranmer?

SUFFOLK
64    He is returned in his opinions, which
      Have satisfied the king for his divorce,
      Together with all famous colleges
      Almost in Christendom. Shortly, I believe,
68    His second marriage shall be published and
      Her coronation. Katherine no more
70    Shall be called queen, but princess dowager,
      And widow to Prince Arthur.

NORFOLK                          This same Cranmer's
72    A worthy fellow, and hath ta'en much pain
      In the king's business.

SUFFOLK                  He has, and we shall see him
      For it an archbishop.

---

52 *memorized* memorialized, long remembered   53 *Digest* i.e., "stomach,"
tolerate   59 *Is posted* has gone posthaste   61 *Ha* (the king's favorite exclamation)   64 *is . . . opinions* (1) is of the same opinion as before (?), (2) has
gathered opinions abroad in support of the king's position (?)   68 *published*
announced   72 *pain* i.e., pains

NORFOLK                    So I hear.
SUFFOLK                              'Tis so.
    *Enter Wolsey and Cromwell.*
  The cardinal!
NORFOLK          Observe, observe, he's moody.
WOLSEY
  The packet, Cromwell,
  Gave't you the king?
CROMWELL                To his own hand, in's bedchamber.
WOLSEY
  Looked he o' th' inside of the paper?                                78
CROMWELL                              Presently
  He did unseal them, and the first he viewed,
  He did it with a serious mind; a heed                             80
  Was in his countenance. You he bade
  Attend him here this morning.
WOLSEY                              Is he ready
  To come abroad?
CROMWELL          I think by this he is.
WOLSEY
  Leave me awhile.                    *Exit Cromwell.*
    *[Aside]*
  It shall be to the Duchess of Alençon,
  The French king's sister; he shall marry her.
  Anne Bullen? No! I'll no Anne Bullens for him;
  There's more in't than fair visage. Bullen?
  No, we'll no Bullens! Speedily I wish
  To hear from Rome. The Marchioness of Pembroke?    90
NORFOLK
  He's discontented.
SUFFOLK              May be he hears the king
  Does whet his anger to him.
SURREY                            Sharp enough,
  Lord, for thy justice!

---

78 *paper* wrapper

WOLSEY   *[Aside]*
    The late queen's gentlewoman? A knight's daughter
    To be her mistress' mistress? The queen's queen?
    This candle burns not clear, 'tis I must snuff it,
    Then out it goes. What though I know her virtuous
    And well-deserving? Yet I know her for
99   A spleeny Lutheran, and not wholesome to
100  Our cause that she should lie i' th' bosom of
101  Our hard-ruled king. Again there is sprung up
102  An heretic, an arch one – Cranmer – one
103  Hath crawled into the favor of the king
104  And is his oracle.
NORFOLK                    He is vexed at something.
        *Enter King, reading of a schedule [, and Lovell].*

SURREY
105  I would 'twere something that would fret the string,
106  The master cord on's heart.
SUFFOLK                                    The king, the king!
KING
    What piles of wealth hath he accumulated
108  To his own portion! And what expense by th' hour
    Seems to flow from him! How i' th' name of thrift
*110*  Does he rake this together? – Now, my lords,
    Saw you the cardinal?
NORFOLK                    My lord, we have
112  Stood here observing him. Some strange commotion
    Is in his brain. He bites his lip, and starts,
    Stops on a sudden, looks upon the ground,
    Then lays his finger on his temple; straight
    Springs out into fast gait, then stops again,

---

**99** *spleeny* passionate; *wholesome* beneficial (*Our cause,* l. 100, being both Wolsey's own and that of the Catholic church)   **100** *lie i' th' bosom of* (1) be the confidante of, (2) be married to   **101** *hard-ruled* hard-to-manage   **102** *arch* chief   **103** *Hath* who has   **104** *oracle* i.e., most influential counselor; **s.d.** *schedule* scroll   **105** *fret the string* corrode (with pun on the "fret" of a stringed instrument)   **106** *on's* of his   **108** *portion* share; *expense* prodigal expenditure   **112** *commotion* upset

Strikes his breast hard, and anon he casts
His eye against the moon. In most strange postures        118
We have seen him set himself.
KING                                   It may well be,
There is a mutiny in's mind. This morning                  120
Papers of state he sent me to peruse
As I required, and wot you what I found                    122
There, on my conscience, put unwittingly?
Forsooth an inventory, thus importing                      124
The several parcels of his plate, his treasure,           125
Rich stuffs and ornaments of household, which
I find at such proud rate that it outspeaks               127
Possession of a subject.
NORFOLK                      It's heaven's will.
Some spirit put this paper in the packet
To bless your eye withal.                                  130
KING                        If we did think
His contemplation were above the earth
And fixed on spiritual object, he should still
Dwell in his musings; but I am afraid
His thinkings are below the moon, not worth               134
His serious considering.
    *King takes his seat; whispers [to] Lovell, who goes to*
    *the Cardinal.*
WOLSEY                          Heaven forgive me;
Even God bless your highness!
KING                            Good my lord,
You are full of heavenly stuff, and bear the inventory    137
Of your best graces in your mind; the which
You were now running o'er. You have scarce time
To steal from spiritual leisure a brief span              140
To keep your earthly audit. Sure in that

---

118 *against* toward   122 *wot* know   124 *importing* indicating   125 *several parcels* separate items   127–28 *outspeaks . . . subject* enumerates more than is appropriate for a subject to own   130 *withal* therewith   134 *below the moon* worldly   137 *stuff* goods   140 *spiritual leisure* time devoted to religious duties or reflections

142    I deem you an ill husband, and am glad
       To have you therein my companion.

WOLSEY                         Sir,
       For holy offices I have a time; a time
       To think upon the part of business which
       I bear i' th' state; and nature does require
147    Her times of preservation, which perforce
       I, her frail son, amongst my brethren mortal,
149    Must give my tendance to.

KING                    You have said well.

WOLSEY
150    And ever may your highness yoke together
       (As I will lend you cause) my doing well
       With my well saying!

KING              'Tis well said again,
       And 'tis a kind of good deed to say well;
       And yet words are no deeds. My father loved you;
155    He said he did, and with his deed did crown
       His word upon you. Since I had my office,
       I have kept you next my heart; have not alone
       Employed you where high profits might come home,
159    But pared my present havings to bestow
160    My bounties upon you.

WOLSEY   *[Aside]*       What should this mean?

SURREY   *[Aside]*
       The Lord increase this business!

KING                 Have I not made you
162    The prime man of the state? I pray you tell me
163    If what I now pronounce you have found true.
164    And if you may confess it, say withal
       If you are bound to us or no. What say you?

---

142 *ill husband* bad manager  147 *preservation* i.e., rest and recovery  149 *tendance* attention  155 *crown* i.e., nobly fulfill  159 *pared* skimped (like paring the cheese down to the rind); *havings* possessions  162 *prime* principal  163 *pronounce* declare  164 *withal* in addition

WOLSEY
My sovereign, I confess your royal graces,
Showered on me daily, have been more than could
My studied purposes requite, which went                    168
Beyond all man's endeavors. My endeavors
Have ever come too short of my desires,                    170
Yet filled with my abilities. Mine own ends                171
Have been mine so, that evermore they pointed             172
To th' good of your most sacred person and
The profit of the state. For your great graces
Heaped upon me (poor undeserver) I
Can nothing render but allegiant thanks,
My prayers to heaven for you, my loyalty,
Which ever has and ever shall be growing,
Till death (that winter) kill it.                          179
KING                              Fairly answered:
A loyal and obedient subject is                           180
Therein illustrated. The honor of it                      181
Does pay the act of it, as i' th' contrary
The foulness is the punishment. I presume                 183
That, as my hand has opened bounty to you,                184
My heart dropped love, my pow'r rained honor, more
On you than any, so your hand and heart,
Your brain and every function of your power
Should, notwithstanding that your bond of duty,           188
As 'twere in love's particular, be more                   189
To me, your friend, than any.                             190
WOLSEY                          I do profess
That for your highness' good I ever labored

---

**168** *studied purposes* deliberate efforts    **171** *filled . . . abilities* i.e., conducted
to the best of my ability    **172** *so* in such a way    **179** *Fairly* finely, deferen-
tially    **181–82** *The honor . . . it* the honor of being loyal is the reward of loyalty    **183** *foulness* i.e., shameful blot    **184** *opened* generously made available
**188** *that* i.e., that particular thing; *bond . . . duty* (Wolsey's obligation to the
pope)    **189** *particular* i.e., special intimacy and obligation

192    More than mine own; that am, have, and will be –
Though all the world should crack their duty to you
And throw it from their soul; though perils did
Abound as thick as thought could make 'em and
Appear in forms more horrid – yet my duty,
197    As doth a rock against the chiding flood,
198    Should the approach of this wild river break,
And stand unshaken yours.

KING                    'Tis nobly spoken.
200    Take notice, lords, he has a loyal breast,
For you have seen him open't. Read o'er this,
*[Gives him papers.]*
And after, this, and then to breakfast with
What appetite you have.

*Exit King frowning upon the Cardinal.*
*The Nobles throng after him, smiling and whispering.*

WOLSEY             What should this mean?
What sudden anger's this? How have I reaped it?
He parted frowning from me, as if ruin
206    Leaped from his eyes. So looks the chafèd lion
207    Upon the daring huntsman that has galled him,
208    Then makes him nothing. I must read this paper;
I fear, the story of his anger. 'Tis so.
210    This paper has undone me. 'Tis th' account
Of all that world of wealth I have drawn together
For mine own ends – indeed to gain the popedom
And fee my friends in Rome. O negligence
214    Fit for a fool to fall by! What cross devil
215    Made me put this main secret in the packet
I sent the king? Is there no way to cure this?
No new device to beat this from his brains?
I know 'twill stir him strongly; yet I know

---

192 *have* have been   197 *chiding* i.e., noisily turbulent   198 *break* withstand (as in "breakwater")   206 *chafèd* enraged   207 *galled* wounded   208 *makes . . . nothing* annihilates him   214 *cross* thwarting   215 *main* principal, vitally important

A way, if it take right, in spite of fortune,                      219
Will bring me off again. What's this? "To th' pope"?              220
The letter (as I live) with all the business
I writ to's holiness. Nay then, farewell!
I have touched the highest point of all my greatness,
And from that full meridian of my glory                           224
I haste now to my setting. I shall fall
Like a bright exhalation in the evening,                          226
And no man see me more.
    *Enter to Wolsey the Dukes of Norfolk and Suffolk, the*
    *Earl of Surrey, and the Lord Chamberlain.*

NORFOLK
Hear the king's pleasure, cardinal, who commands you
To render up the great seal presently                             229
Into our hands and to confine yourself                            230
To Asher House, my Lord of Winchester's,
Till you hear further from his highness.

WOLSEY                                        Stay!
Where's your commission, lords? Words cannot carry                233
Authority so weighty.                                             234

SUFFOLK                        Who dare cross 'em,
Bearing the king's will from his mouth expressly?

WOLSEY
Till I find more than will or words to do it                      236
(I mean your malice) know, officious lords,
I dare and must deny it. Now I feel
Of what coarse metal ye are molded, envy,                         239
How eagerly ye follow my disgraces                                240
As if it fed ye, and how sleek and wanton                         241
Ye appear in everything may bring my ruin!
Follow your envious courses, men of malice.
You have Christian warrant for 'em, and no doubt                  244

---

**219** *take right* succeed  **220** *bring me off* rescue me, exonerate me  **224** *full meridian* apogee  **226** *exhalation* meteor (metaphoric allusion to the fall of Lucifer)  **229** *presently* immediately  **233** *commission* written authority  **234** *cross* oppose  **236** *do it* i.e., relinquish my authority  **239** *envy* malice  **241** *wanton* headlong, shamefully eager  **244** *Christian warrant* (ironic)

245   In time will find their fit rewards. That seal
      You ask with such a violence, the king
      (Mine and your master) with his own hand gave me,
248   Bade me enjoy it, with the place and honors,
      During my life, and to confirm his goodness
250   Ties it by letters patents. Now who'll take it?
SURREY
      The king that gave it.
WOLSEY                          It must be himself then.
SURREY
      Thou art a proud traitor, priest.
WOLSEY                              Proud lord, thou liest!
253   Within these forty hours Surrey durst better
      Have burnt that tongue than said so.
SURREY                                      Thy ambition
255   (Thou scarlet sin) robbed this bewailing land
      Of noble Buckingham, my father-in-law.
      The heads of all thy brother cardinals
258   (With thee and all thy best parts bound together)
259   Weighed not a hair of his. Plague of your policy!
260   You sent me Deputy for Ireland,
      Far from his succor, from the king, from all
262   That might have mercy on the fault thou gav'st him,
      Whilst your great goodness, out of holy pity,
      Absolved him with an ax.
WOLSEY                          This, and all else
265   This talking lord can lay upon my credit,
      I answer is most false. The duke by law
      Found his deserts. How innocent I was
268   From any private malice in his end,
      His noble jury and foul cause can witness.
270   If I loved many words, lord, I should tell you

---

245 *find* meet with   248 *place* position (of Lord Chancellor)   250 *letters patents* open (public) documents   253 *forty hours* (a round number)   255 *scarlet* (alluding both to the robes of a cardinal and the heinousness of the sin)   258 *parts* qualities   259 *policy* conniving   262 *fault* offense; *gav'st him* accused him of   265 *credit* good name   268 *From* of

You have as little honesty as honor,
That in the way of loyalty and truth                              272
Toward the king, my ever royal master,
Dare mate a sounder man than Surrey can be                       274
And all that love his follies.
SURREY                              By my soul,
    Your long coat, priest, protects you; thou shouldst feel
    My sword i' th' lifeblood of thee else. My lords,
    Can ye endure to hear this arrogance?
    And from this fellow? If we live thus tamely,               279
    To be thus jaded by a piece of scarlet,                     280
    Farewell nobility: let his grace go forward
    And dare us with his cap, like larks.                       282
WOLSEY                                      All goodness
    Is poison to thy stomach.
SURREY                              Yes, that goodness
    Of gleaning all the land's wealth into one,
    Into your own hands, cardinal, by extortion;
    The goodness of your intercepted packets
    You writ to th' pope against the king. Your goodness,
    Since you provoke me, shall be most notorious.              288
    My Lord of Norfolk, as you are truly noble,
    As you respect the common good, the state                   290
    Of our despised nobility, our issues                        291
    (Whom, if he live, will scarce be gentlemen),
    Produce the grand sum of his sins, the articles             293
    Collected from his life. I'll startle you
    Worse than the sacring bell when the brown wench            295
    Lay kissing in your arms, lord cardinal.

---

272 *That* I that   274 *mate* match   279 *tamely* meekly   280 *jaded* cowed,
humiliated   282 *dare* dazzle (alludes to a method of catching larks with the
help of a mirror and red cloth)   288 *notorious* openly known   291 *issues*
male heirs   293 *articles* counts of indictment   295 *sacring bell* bell sum-
moning to prayers; *brown wench* (implying a sunburned slut from the lower
classes, gentry women supposedly being characterized by their fair, protected
skins)

WOLSEY
    How much, methinks, I could despise this man
    But that I am bound in charity against it.
NORFOLK
    Those articles, my lord, are in the king's hand.
300    But thus much – they are foul ones.
WOLSEY                                           So much fairer
    And spotless shall mine innocence arise
    When the king knows my truth.
SURREY                                           This cannot save you.
    I thank my memory, I yet remember
    Some of these articles, and out they shall!
    Now if you can blush and cry guilty, cardinal,
    You'll show a little honesty.
WOLSEY                                   Speak on, sir,
307    I dare your worst objections. If I blush,
    It is to see a nobleman want manners.
SURREY
309    I had rather want those than my head. Have at you!
*310*    First, that without the king's assent or knowledge
311    You wrought to be a legate, by which power
    You maimed the jurisdiction of all bishops.
NORFOLK
    Then, that all you writ to Rome, or else
314    To foreign princes, *"Ego et Rex meus"*
315    Was still inscribed, in which you brought the king
    To be your servant.
SUFFOLK                        Then, that without the knowledge
    Either of king or council, when you went
318    Ambassador to the emperor, you made bold
    To carry into Flanders the great seal.

---

300 *thus much* i.e., I can tell you this much   307 *objections* accusations
309 *Have at you* (phrase of challenge or imminent attack)   311 *wrought*
contrived; *legate* pope's official representative   314 *Ego . . . meus* I and my
king   315 *still* always   318 *emperor* i.e., Charles V

SURREY
　　Item, you sent a large commission                          320
　　To Gregory de Cassado to conclude,
　　Without the king's will or the state's allowance,           322
　　A league between his highness and Ferrara.

SUFFOLK
　　That out of mere ambition you have caused                   324
　　Your holy hat to be stamped on the king's coin.             325

SURREY
　　Then, that you have sent innumerable substance              326
　　(By what means got, I leave to your own conscience)
　　To furnish Rome and to prepare the ways                     328
　　You have for dignities, to the mere undoing                 329
　　Of all the kingdom. Many more there are,                    330
　　Which, since they are of you, and odious,
　　I will not taint my mouth with.

CHAMBERLAIN                               O my lord,
　　Press not a falling man too far! 'Tis virtue.
　　His faults lie open to the laws; let them,
　　Not you, correct him. My heart weeps to see him
　　So little of his great self.

SURREY                              I forgive him.

SUFFOLK
　　Lord cardinal, the king's further pleasure is –
　　Because all those things you have done of late
　　By your power legative within this kingdom                  339
　　Fall into th' compass of a praemunire –                     340
　　That therefore such a writ be sued against you,             341
　　To forfeit all your goods, lands, tenements,

---

322 *allowance* permission   324 *mere* sheer   325 *Your . . . coin* (Wolsey had
illegitimately caused his image to be imprinted on the coins known as groats)
326 *innumerable substance* countless wealth   328 *furnish* supply   329 *dignities* honors; *mere undoing* utter ruin   339 *legative* as legate   340 *compass*
scope; *praemunire* writ by which a person was charged with asserting papal
jurisdiction in England, thus preempting royal authority   341 *sued* applied
for

Chattels, and whatsoever, and to be
344    Out of the king's protection. This is my charge.

NORFOLK

And so we'll leave you to your meditations
How to live better. For your stubborn answer
About the giving back the great seal to us,
The king shall know it, and (no doubt) shall thank you.
349    So fare you well, my little good lord cardinal.

*Exeunt all but Wolsey.*

WOLSEY

350    So farewell to the little good you bear me.
Farewell? A long farewell to all my greatness!
This is the state of man: today he puts forth
The tender leaves of hopes; tomorrow blossoms
354    And bears his blushing honors thick upon him;
The third day comes a frost, a killing frost,
356    And when he thinks, good easy man, full surely
His greatness is a-ripening, nips his root,
And then he falls as I do. I have ventured,
359    Like little wanton boys that swim on bladders,
360    This many summers in a sea of glory,
But far beyond my depth. My high-blown pride
At length broke under me, and now has left me,
Weary and old with service, to the mercy
364    Of a rude stream that must for ever hide me.
Vain pomp and glory of this world, I hate ye!
I feel my heart new opened. O, how wretched
Is that poor man that hangs on princes' favors!
There is betwixt that smile we would aspire to,
369    That sweet aspect of princes, and their ruin,
370    More pangs and fears than wars or women have;
And when he falls, he falls like Lucifer,

---

344 *Out . . . protection* i.e., without legal protection   349 *little good* (playing
on the conventional salutation "my good lord")   354 *blushing* glowing
356 *easy* comfortable, easygoing   359 *wanton* reckless   364 *rude* rough
369 *their ruin* the ruin they cause

Never to hope again.
> *Enter Cromwell, standing amazed.*
                              Why how now, Cromwell?

CROMWELL
  I have no power to speak, sir.

WOLSEY                              What, amazed
  At my misfortunes? Can thy spirit wonder
  A great man should decline? Nay, an you weep,           375
  I am fall'n indeed.

CROMWELL              How does your grace?

WOLSEY                                        Why well;
  Never so truly happy, my good Cromwell.
  I know myself now, and I feel within me
  A peace above all earthly dignities,
  A still and quiet conscience. The king has cured me –    380
  I humbly thank his grace – and from these shoulders,
  These ruined pillars, out of pity taken
  A load would sink a navy, too much honor.
  O 'tis a burden, Cromwell, 'tis a burden
  Too heavy for a man that hopes for heaven.

CROMWELL
  I am glad your grace has made that right use of it.

WOLSEY
  I hope I have. I am able now, methinks,
  Out of a fortitude of soul I feel,
  To endure more miseries and greater far
  Than my weakhearted enemies dare offer.                  390
  What news abroad?

CROMWELL            The heaviest and the worst
  Is your displeasure with the king.                       392

WOLSEY                              God bless him!

CROMWELL
  The next is that Sir Thomas More is chosen
  Lord Chancellor in your place.

WOLSEY                              That's somewhat sudden.

---

375 *an* if   392 *your . . . king* i.e., the king's displeasure with you

But he's a learnèd man. May he continue
Long in his highness' favor, and do justice
For truth's sake and his conscience; that his bones,
When he has run his course and sleeps in blessings,
399 May have a tomb of orphans' tears wept on him.
400 What more?

CROMWELL    That Cranmer is returned with welcome;
Installed Lord Archbishop of Canterbury.

WOLSEY
That's news indeed.

CROMWELL                Last, that the Lady Anne,
Whom the king hath in secrecy long married,
This day was viewed in open as his queen,
405 Going to chapel; and the voice is now
Only about her coronation.

WOLSEY
There was the weight that pulled me down. O
    Cromwell,
408 The king has gone beyond me. All my glories
In that one woman I have lost for ever.
410 No sun shall ever usher forth mine honors
411 Or gild again the noble troops that waited
Upon my smiles. Go get thee from me, Cromwell!
I am a poor fall'n man, unworthy now
To be thy lord and master. Seek the king
(That sun, I pray, may never set). I have told him
What and how true thou art. He will advance thee.
Some little memory of me will stir him
(I know his noble nature) not to let
Thy hopeful service perish too. Good Cromwell,
420 Neglect him not; make use now, and provide
For thine own future safety.

CROMWELL                            O my lord,

---

399 *a tomb . . . him* (the Lord Chancellor was legal guardian of orphaned
children)   405 *voice* general talk   408 *gone beyond* outstripped, overreached
411 *troops* retainers   420 *make use* take advantage

Must I then leave you? Must I needs forgo
So good, so noble, and so true a master?
Bear witness, all that have not hearts of iron,
With what a sorrow Cromwell leaves his lord.
The king shall have my service, but my pray'rs
For ever and for ever shall be yours.

WOLSEY

Cromwell, I did not think to shed a tear
In all my miseries, but thou hast forced me
(Out of thy honest truth) to play the woman.                430
Let's dry our eyes, and thus far hear me, Cromwell,
And when I am forgotten, as I shall be,
And sleep in dull cold marble, where no mention
Of me more must be heard of, say I taught thee.
Say Wolsey, that once trod the ways of glory
And sounded all the depths and shoals of honor,           436
Found thee a way (out of his wrack) to rise in,           437
A sure and safe one, though thy master missed it.
Mark but my fall and that that ruined me.
Cromwell, I charge thee, fling away ambition!             440
By that sin fell the angels; how can man then
(The image of his Maker) hope to win by it?               442
Love thyself last, cherish those hearts that hate thee;
Corruption wins not more than honesty.
Still in thy right hand carry gentle peace                445
To silence envious tongues. Be just, and fear not.
Let all the ends thou aim'st at be thy country's,
Thy God's, and truth's. Then if thou fall'st, O Cromwell,
Thou fall'st a blessed martyr.
Serve the king. And prithee lead me in,                   450
There take an inventory of all I have
To the last penny: 'tis the king's. My robe
And my integrity to heaven is all

---

430 *truth* loyalty  436 *shoals* shallows  437 *wrack* shipwreck  442 *win* profit  445 *Still* constantly

I dare now call mine own. O Cromwell, Cromwell,
Had I but served my God with half the zeal
I served my king, he would not in mine age
457   Have left me naked to mine enemies.

CROMWELL
Good sir, have patience.

WOLSEY                  So I have. Farewell
The hopes of court; my hopes in heaven do dwell.

                                     *Exeunt.*

\*

&#126; **IV.1** *Enter two Gentlemen, meeting one another.*

FIRST GENTLEMAN
You're well met once again.

SECOND GENTLEMAN              So are you.

FIRST GENTLEMAN
You come to take your stand here, and behold
The Lady Anne pass from her coronation?

SECOND GENTLEMAN
'Tis all my business. At our last encounter
The Duke of Buckingham came from his trial.

FIRST GENTLEMAN
'Tis very true, but that time offered sorrow,
This, general joy.

SECOND GENTLEMAN
                   'Tis well. The citizens
8   I am sure have shown at full their royal minds –
9   As let 'em have their rights, they are ever forward –
10   In celebration of this day with shows,
Pageants, and sights of honor.

---

457 *naked* defenseless
     IV.1 A street in Westminster   8 *royal minds* devotion to royalty   9 *As let . . . rights* to give them their due

FIRST GENTLEMAN                     Never greater,
  Nor, I'll assure you, better taken, sir.                            12
SECOND GENTLEMAN
  May I be bold to ask what that contains,
  That paper in your hand?
FIRST GENTLEMAN                Yes, 'tis the list
  Of those that claim their offices this day,
  By custom of the coronation.
  The Duke of Suffolk is the first, and claims
  To be high steward; next, the Duke of Norfolk,
  He to be earl marshal. You may read the rest.
SECOND GENTLEMAN
  I thank you, sir. Had I not known those customs,           20
  I should have been beholding to your paper.               21
  But, I beseech you, what's become of Katherine,
  The princess dowager? How goes her business?
FIRST GENTLEMAN
  That I can tell you too. The Archbishop
  Of Canterbury, accompanied with other
  Learnèd and reverend fathers of his order,
  Held a late court at Dunstable, six miles off           27
  From Ampthill, where the princess lay, to which         28
  She was often cited by them, but appeared not;          29
  And to be short, for not-appearance and                 30
  The king's late scruple, by the main assent             31
  Of all these learned men she was divorced
  And the late marriage made of none effect,              33
  Since which she was removed to Kimbolton,
  Where she remains now sick.
SECOND GENTLEMAN              Alas good lady.
    [Trumpets.]

---

12 *taken* appreciated   21 *beholding* indebted   27 *late* recent   28 *lay* resided
29 *cited* summoned   31 *late* former; *main assent* consensus   33 *made of
none effect* annulled

36    The trumpets sound. Stand close, the queen is coming.
       *Hautboys.*

                    *The Order of the Coronation*
          1. *A lively flourish of trumpets.*
          2. *Then two Judges.*
          3. *Lord Chancellor, with purse and mace before him.*
          4. *Choristers singing. Music.*
          5. *Mayor of London, bearing the mace. Then Garter,*
             *in his coat of arms, and on his head he wore a gilt*
             *copper crown.*
          6. *Marquis Dorset, bearing a scepter of gold, on his*
             *head a demicoronal of gold. With him the Earl of*
             *Surrey, bearing the rod of silver with the dove,*
             *crowned with an earl's coronet. Collars of Esses.*
          7. *Duke of Suffolk, in his robe of estate, his coronet on*
             *his head, bearing a long white wand, as high*
             *steward. With him the Duke of Norfolk, with the*
             *rod of marshalship, a coronet on his head. Collars of*
             *Esses.*
          8. *A canopy borne by four of the Cinque Ports; under*
             *it the Queen in her robe; in her hair, richly*
             *adorned with pearl, crowned. On each side her the*
             *Bishops of London and Winchester.*
          9. *The old Duchess of Norfolk, in a coronal of gold,*
             *wrought with flowers, bearing the Queen's train.*
         10. *Certain Ladies or Countesses, with plain circlets of*
             *gold without flowers.*
                           *Exeunt, first passing over the stage*
                               *in order and state, and then*
                               *a great flourish of trumpets.*

---

**36 s.d.** *Hautboys* early form of oboe; **item 3** *Lord Chancellor* (now Sir
Thomas More); **item 5** *Garter* the chief herald, known as the Garter King-
of-Arms; **item 6** *demicoronal* small, crownlike circlet; **items 6, 7** *Collars of
Esses* ornamental chains made with linked letters "S"; **item 7** *estate* state; **item
8** *Cinque Ports* barons of the five Channel ports of Hastings, Sandwich,
Dover, Romney, and Hythe; *in her hair* with her hair hanging loose (customary for brides)

SECOND GENTLEMAN
    A royal train, believe me. These I know.                                                37
    Who's that that bears the scepter?
FIRST GENTLEMAN                Marquis Dorset,
    And that the Earl of Surrey with the rod.
SECOND GENTLEMAN
    A bold brave gentleman. That should be                                                40
    The Duke of Suffolk.
FIRST GENTLEMAN       'Tis the same: high steward.
SECOND GENTLEMAN
    And that my Lord of Norfolk?
FIRST GENTLEMAN          Yes.
SECOND GENTLEMAN *[Looks on the Queen.]* Heaven bless
    thee,
    Thou hast the sweetest face I ever looked on.
    Sir, as I have a soul, she is an angel;
    Our king has all the Indies in his arms,                                                45
    And more, and richer, when he strains that lady.                                          46
    I cannot blame his conscience.
FIRST GENTLEMAN           They that bear
    The cloth of honor over her are four barons                                              48
    Of the Cinque Ports.
SECOND GENTLEMAN
    Those men are happy, and so are all are near her.                                         50
    I take it, she that carries up the train                                                 51
    Is that old noble lady, Duchess of Norfolk.
FIRST GENTLEMAN
    It is, and all the rest are countesses.
SECOND GENTLEMAN
    Their coronets say so. These are stars indeed –                                          54
FIRST GENTLEMAN
    And sometimes falling ones.                                                               55

---

**37** *train* retinue   **45** *Indies* i.e., limitless riches (both the East and West Indies were regarded as sources of wealth)   **46** *strains* embraces, makes love to **48** *cloth of honor* canopy   **50** *all* all who   **51** *carries . . . train* bears Anne's long robe   **54** *stars* (term for the nobility)   **55** *falling* (with sexual innuendo)

SECOND GENTLEMAN                    No more of that.
                                        *[Exit procession.]*
    *Enter a third Gentleman.*
FIRST GENTLEMAN
    God save you, sir. Where have you been broiling?
THIRD GENTLEMAN
57    Among the crowd i' th' Abbey, where a finger
    Could not be wedged in more. I am stifled
59    With the mere rankness of their joy.
SECOND GENTLEMAN                          You saw
60    The ceremony?
THIRD GENTLEMAN    That I did.
FIRST GENTLEMAN                     How was it?
THIRD GENTLEMAN
61    Well worth the seeing.
SECOND GENTLEMAN    Good sir, speak it to us.
THIRD GENTLEMAN
    As well as I am able. The rich stream
    Of lords and ladies, having brought the queen
64    To a prepared place in the choir, fell off
    A distance from her, while her grace sat down
    To rest awhile, some half an hour or so,
67    In a rich chair of state, opposing freely
    The beauty of her person to the people.
69    Believe me, sir, she is the goodliest woman
70    That ever lay by man; which when the people
    Had the full view of, such a noise arose
72    As the shrouds make at sea in a stiff tempest,
    As loud, and to as many tunes. Hats, cloaks
74    (Doublets, I think) flew up; and had their faces
    Been loose, this day they had been lost. Such joy
    I never saw before. Great-bellied women

---

57 *th' Abbey* Westminster Abbey (scene of the coronation)    59 *mere rankness*
sheer exuberance (with possible allusion to the smell of the crowd)    61 *speak*
describe    64 *fell off* withdrew    67 *opposing* exposing    69 *goodliest* best-look-
ing    72 *shrouds* sail ropes    74 *Doublets* close-fitting body garments worn by
men

That had not half a week to go, like rams                    77
In the old time of war, would shake the press                78
And make 'em reel before 'em. No man living
Could say "This is my wife" there, all were woven            80
So strangely in one piece.                                    81
SECOND GENTLEMAN            But what followed?
THIRD GENTLEMAN
At length her grace rose and with modest paces               82
Came to the altar, where she kneeled, and saintlike
Cast her fair eyes to heaven and prayed devoutly,
Then rose again and bowed her to the people,
When by the Archbishop of Canterbury
She had all the royal makings of a queen,                    87
As holy oil, Edward Confessor's crown,                       88
The rod, and bird of peace, and all such emblems
Laid nobly on her; which performed, the choir               90
With all the choicest music of the kingdom                   91
Together sung "Te Deum." So she parted,                      92
And with the same full state packed back again               93
To York Place, where the feast is held.
FIRST GENTLEMAN                            Sir,
You must no more call it York Place. That's past,
For since the cardinal fell that title's lost;
'Tis now the king's, and called Whitehall.
THIRD GENTLEMAN                           I know it,
But 'tis so lately altered that the old name
Is fresh about me.
SECOND GENTLEMAN  What two reverend bishops
Were those that went on each side of the queen?              100
THIRD GENTLEMAN
Stokely and Gardiner, the one of Winchester,
Newly preferred from the king's secretary,                   102

---

77 *rams* battering-rams   78 *shake the press* jostle the crowd   81 *piece* (of fabric)   82 *modest* moderate   87 *makings* accoutrements   88 *As* namely   91
*music* musicians   92 *Te Deum* thee, God (we praise); *parted* departed   93
*state* pomp; *packed* proceeded   102 *preferred* advanced

The other, London.

SECOND GENTLEMAN  He of Winchester
Is held no great good lover of the archbishop's,
The virtuous Cranmer.

THIRD GENTLEMAN       All the land knows that.
However, yet there is no great breach. When it comes,
Cranmer will find a friend will not shrink from him.

SECOND GENTLEMAN
Who may that be, I pray you?

THIRD GENTLEMAN              Thomas Cromwell,
A man in much esteem with th' king, and truly
110    A worthy friend. The king has made him
111    Master o' th' Jewel House,
And one, already, of the Privy Council.

SECOND GENTLEMAN
He will deserve more.

THIRD GENTLEMAN      Yes, without all doubt.
Come, gentlemen, ye shall go my way,
Which is to th' court, and there ye shall be my guests.
116    Something I can command. As I walk thither,
I'll tell ye more.

BOTH              You may command us, sir.      *Exeunt.*

*

∾ **IV.2**  *Enter Katherine Dowager, sick, led between
Griffith, her gentleman usher, and Patience, her
woman.*

GRIFFITH
How does your grace?

KATHERINE              O Griffith, sick to death.
My legs like loaden branches bow to th' earth,
Willing to leave their burden. Reach a chair.

---

111 *Master o' th' Jewel House* keeper of the crown jewels, royal treasure, etc.
116 *Something . . . command* i.e., I can scratch up something to eat
   **IV.2** Katherine's apartments (at Kimbolton)

So now, methinks, I feel a little ease.
Didst thou not tell me, Griffith, as thou led'st me,
That the great child of honor, Cardinal Wolsey,          6
Was dead?
GRIFFITH      Yes, madam, but I think your grace,
Out of the pain you suffered, gave no ear to't.
KATHERINE
Prithee, good Griffith, tell me how he died.
If well, he stepped before me happily                    10
For my example.                                          11
GRIFFITH              Well, the voice goes, madam,
For after the stout Earl Northumberland                  12
Arrested him at York and brought him forward
As a man sorely tainted, to his answer,                  14
He fell sick suddenly, and grew so ill
He could not sit his mule.
KATHERINE                        Alas, poor man.
GRIFFITH
At last, with easy roads, he came to Leicester,          17
Lodged in the abbey, where the reverend abbot
With all his covent honorably received him,              19
To whom he gave these words: "O father abbot,            20
An old man, broken with the storms of state,
Is come to lay his weary bones among ye.
Give him a little earth for charity!"
So went to bed, where eagerly his sickness
Pursued him still, and three nights after this,
After the hour of eight, which he himself
Foretold should be his last, full of repentance,
Continual meditations, tears and sorrows,                28
He gave his honors to the world again,
His blessèd part to heaven, and slept in peace.          30

---

**6** *child of honor* (normally refers to one of noble birth; here ironic?)   **10** *happily* (1) perhaps, (2) fortunately   **11** *voice* common talk   **12** *stout* (1) strong, (2) haughty   **14** *sorely tainted* severely discredited   **17** *roads* stages of a journey   **19** *covent* convent   **28** *sorrows* expressions of sorrow   **30** *blessèd part* i.e., soul

KATHERINE
  So may he rest, his faults lie gently on him!
32  Yet thus far, Griffith, give me leave to speak him,
  And yet with charity. He was a man
34  Of an unbounded stomach, ever ranking
35  Himself with princes; one that by suggestion
36  Tied all the kingdom. Simony was fair play;
37  His own opinion was his law. I' th' presence
38  He would say untruths, and be ever double
  Both in his words and meaning. He was never
40  (But where he meant to ruin) pitiful.
  His promises were, as he then was, mighty;
  But his performance, as he is now, nothing.
43  Of his own body he was ill, and gave
  The clergy ill example.
GRIFFITH                    Noble madam,
  Men's evil manners live in brass; their virtues
  We write in water. May it please your highness
  To hear me speak his good now?
KATHERINE                      Yes, good Griffith,
  I were malicious else.
GRIFFITH                This cardinal,
  Though from an humble stock, undoubtedly
50  Was fashioned to much honor. From his cradle
51  He was a scholar, and a ripe and good one,
  Exceeding wise, fair-spoken, and persuading;
53  Lofty and sour to them that loved him not,
  But to those men that sought him, sweet as summer.
  And though he were unsatisfied in getting
  (Which was a sin), yet in bestowing, madam,
  He was most princely. Ever witness for him
58  Those twins of learning that he raised in you,

---

32 *speak* describe   34 *unbounded stomach* limitless ambition   35 *suggestion*
double-dealing   36 *Tied* fettered; *Simony* trafficking in church preferments
37 *presence* royal presence chamber   38 *double* deceitful   40 *pitiful* compas-
sionate   43 *ill* corrupt   50 *fashioned to* cut out for   51 *ripe* accomplished
53 *Lofty* haughty   58 *twins of learning* i.e., colleges; *raised* founded

Ipswich and Oxford; one of which fell with him,
Unwilling to outlive the good that did it;                                60
The other, though unfinished, yet so famous,
So excellent in art, and still so rising,                                 62
That Christendom shall ever speak his virtue.
His overthrow heaped happiness upon him,
For then, and not till then, he felt himself,                             65
And found the blessedness of being little.
And, to add greater honors to his age
Than man could give him, he died fearing God.

KATHERINE
After my death I wish no other herald,
No other speaker of my living actions                                     70
To keep mine honor from corruption,
But such an honest chronicler as Griffith.
Whom I most hated living, thou hast made me,
With thy religious truth and modesty,                                     74
Now, in his ashes, honor. Peace be with him!
Patience, be near me still, and set me lower;
I have not long to trouble thee. Good Griffith,
Cause the musicians play me that sad note                                 78
I named my knell, whilst I sit meditating
On that celestial harmony I go to.                                        80
    *Sad and solemn music.*

GRIFFITH
She is asleep. Good wench, let's sit down quiet
For fear we wake her. Softly, gentle Patience.                           82


*The Vision*
*Enter, solemnly tripping one after another, six personages*
*clad in white robes, wearing on their heads garlands of*
*bays, and golden vizards on their faces, branches of bays*
*or palm in their hands. They first congee unto her, then*

---

**60** *good* good man; *did* created   **62** *rising* (both as a building and an influ-
ence)   **65** *felt himself* knew himself   **70** *living* while alive   **74** *modesty* moderation   **78** *note* melody   **82 s.d.** *bays* laurel; *vizards* masks; *congee* bow

> *dance; and, at certain changes, the first two hold a spare*
> *garland over her head; at which the other four make*
> *reverent curtsies. Then the two that held the garland*
> *deliver the same to the other next two, who observe the*
> *same order in their changes, and holding the garland*
> *over her head; which done, they deliver the same*
> *garland to tshe last two, who likewise observe the same*
> *order; at which (as it were by inspiration) she makes (in*
> *her sleep) signs of rejoicing and holdeth up her hands to*
> *heaven. And so in their dancing vanish, carrying the*
> *garland with them. The music continues.*

KATHERINE
　Spirit of peace, where are ye? Are ye all gone
　And leave me here in wretchedness behind ye?

GRIFFITH
　Madam, we are here.

KATHERINE　　　　　　It is not you I call for.
　Saw ye none enter since I slept?

GRIFFITH　　　　　　　　　　None, madam.

KATHERINE
　No? Saw you not even now a blessed troop
　Invite me to a banquet, whose bright faces
　Cast thousand beams upon me like the sun?
90　They promised me eternal happiness
　And brought me garlands, Griffith, which I feel
　I am not worthy yet to wear; I shall assuredly.

GRIFFITH
　I am most joyful, madam, such good dreams
94　Possess your fancy.

KATHERINE　　　　　Bid the music leave.
95　They are harsh and heavy to me.
　　*Music ceases.*

PATIENCE　　　　　　　　　　Do you note

---

82 s.d. (cont'd) *changes* figures in the dance　94 *Possess* occupy; *music* musicians; *leave* cease playing　95 *heavy* oppressive

How much her grace is altered on the sudden?
How long her face is drawn? How pale she looks,
And of an earthly cold? Mark her eyes!                    98

GRIFFITH
She is going, wench. Pray, pray!

PATIENCE                              Heaven comfort her!
        *Enter a Messenger.*

MESSENGER
An't like your grace –                                   100

KATHERINE              You are a saucy fellow!
Deserve we no more reverence?

GRIFFITH                               You are to blame,
Knowing she will not lose her wonted greatness,          102
To use so rude behavior. Go to, kneel!

MESSENGER
I humbly do entreat your highness' pardon;
My haste made me unmannerly. There is staying            105
A gentleman sent from the king, to see you.

KATHERINE
Admit him entrance, Griffith. But this fellow            107
Let me ne'er see again.              *[Exit Messenger].*
        *Enter Lord Capuchius.*
                          If my sight fail not,
You should be lord ambassador from the emperor,
My royal nephew, and your name Capuchius.                110

CAPUCHIUS
Madam, the same. Your servant.

KATHERINE                        O my lord,
The times and titles now are altered strangely
With me since first you knew me. But I pray you,
What is your pleasure with me?

CAPUCHIUS                      Noble lady,
First mine own service to your grace. The next,
The king's request that I would visit you,

_____

98 *cold* coldness (taken as a sign of impending death)  102 *lose* forgo;
*wonted* accustomed  105 *staying* waiting  107 *Admit* allow

Who grieves much for your weakness, and by me
118 Sends you his princely commendations,
And heartily entreats you take good comfort.

KATHERINE
120 O my good lord, that comfort comes too late,
'Tis like a pardon after execution.
122 That gentle physic, given in time, had cured me,
But now I am past all comforts here but prayers.
How does his highness?

CAPUCHIUS                            Madam, in good health.

KATHERINE
So may he ever do, and ever flourish,
When I shall dwell with worms, and my poor name
Banished the kingdom. Patience, is that letter
I caused you write yet sent away?

PATIENCE                            No, madam.
        *[Gives it to Katherine.]*

KATHERINE
Sir, I most humbly pray you to deliver
130 This to my lord the king.

CAPUCHIUS                            Most willing, madam.

KATHERINE
In which I have commended to his goodness
132 The model of our chaste loves, his young daughter –
The dews of heaven fall thick in blessings on her! –
134 Beseeching him to give her virtuous breeding –
She is young and of a noble modest nature;
I hope she will deserve well – and a little
137 To love her for her mother's sake, that loved him,
Heaven knows how dearly. My next poor petition
Is that his noble grace would have some pity
140 Upon my wretched women, that so long
141 Have followed both my fortunes faithfully,
Of which there is not one, I dare avow

---

118 *commendations* compliments   122 *had* would have   132 *model* image,
token; *our* i.e., hers and Henry's   134 *virtuous breeding* good upbringing
and education   137 *him* i.e., Henry   141 *both* i.e., good and bad

(And now I should not lie), but will deserve
For virtue and true beauty of the soul,
For honesty and decent carriage,                            145
A right good husband – let him be a noble –
And sure those men are happy that shall have 'em.
The last is for my men – they are the poorest
But poverty could never draw 'em from me –
That they may have their wages duly paid 'em,              *150*
And something over to remember me by.
If heaven had pleased to have given me longer life
And able means, we had not parted thus.                    153
These are the whole contents. And, good my lord,
By that you love the dearest in this world,
As you wish Christian peace to souls departed,
Stand these poor people's friend, and urge the king        157
To do me this last right.
CAPUCHIUS                       By heaven I will,
Or let me lose the fashion of a man!                       159
KATHERINE
I thank you, honest lord. Remember me                      *160*
In all humility unto his highness.
Say his long trouble now is passing
Out of this world. Tell him in death I blessed him,
For so I will. Mine eyes grow dim. Farewell,
My lord. Griffith, farewell. Nay, Patience,
You must not leave me yet. I must to bed;
Call in more women. When I am dead, good wench,
Let me be used with honor. Strew me over
With maiden flowers, that all the world may know           169
I was a chaste wife to my grave. Embalm me,               *170*
Then lay me forth. Although unqueened, yet like           *171*
A queen, and daughter to a king, inter me.
I can no more.                  *Exeunt, leading Katherine.*

---

145 *decent carriage* proper demeanor    153 *able* sufficient    157 *Stand* remain   159 *fashion* nature, character   169 *maiden flowers* (emblems of
chastity)   171 *lay me forth* lay me out

*

❧ **V.1** *Enter Gardiner, Bishop of Winchester, a Page*
*with a torch before him, met by Sir Thomas Lovell.*

GARDINER
  It's one o'clock, boy, is't not?
BOY                         It hath struck.
GARDINER
  These should be hours for necessities,
3  Not for delights; times to repair our nature
  With comforting repose, and not for us
  To waste these times. Good hour of night, Sir Thomas:
  Whither so late?
LOVELL           Came you from the king, my lord?
GARDINER
7  I did, Sir Thomas, and left him at primero
  With the Duke of Suffolk.
LOVELL            I must to him too
  Before he go to bed. I'll take my leave.
GARDINER
10  Not yet, Sir Thomas Lovell. What's the matter?
11  It seems you are in haste. An if there be
  No great offense belongs to't, give your friend
13  Some touch of your late business. Affairs that walk
  (As they say spirits do) at midnight have
  In them a wilder nature than the business
  That seeks dispatch by day.
LOVELL            My lord, I love you,
17  And durst commend a secret to your ear
  Much weightier than this work. The queen's in labor,
19  They say in great extremity, and feared

---

V.1 The royal palace  **3** *repair* restore  **7** *primero* a gambling card game  **11**
*An if* if truly  **13** *touch* hint; *walk* continue  **17** *commend* entrust  **19**
*feared* i.e., it is feared that

She'll with the labor end.                                       20

GARDINER                The fruit she goes with
I pray for heartily, that it may find
Good time, and live. But for the stock, Sir Thomas,             22
I wish it grubbed up now.                                       23

LOVELL                 Methinks I could
Cry the amen, and yet my conscience says                        24
She's a good creature and sweet lady, does
Deserve our better wishes.

GARDINER              But, sir, sir,
Hear me, Sir Thomas! You're a gentleman
Of mine own way. I know you wise, religious,                    28
And let me tell you it will ne'er be well –
'Twill not, Sir Thomas Lovell, take't of me –                   30
Till Cranmer, Cromwell, her two hands, and she
Sleep in their graves.

LOVELL              Now, sir, you speak of two
The most remarked i' th' kingdom. As for Cromwell,             33
Beside that of the Jewel House, is made Master                 34
O' th' Rolls and the king's secretary; further, sir,
Stands in the gap and trade of more preferments,              36
With which the time will load him. Th' archbishop             37
Is the king's hand and tongue, and who dare speak
One syllable against him?

GARDINER                    Yes, yes, Sir Thomas,
There are that dare, and I myself have ventured               40
To speak my mind of him; and indeed this day,
Sir (I may tell it you), I think I have
Incensed the lords o' th' council that he is                   43
(For so I know he is, they know he is)
A most arch-heretic, a pestilence                             45

---

20 *fruit she goes with* i.e., the child she bears   22 *Good time* good fortune; *the stock,* i.e., the parent   23 *grubbed up* rooted out   24 *Cry the amen* assent   28 *Of mine own way* i.e., of my own Catholic persuasion   33 *remarked* noted, prominent   34–35 *Master . . . Rolls* judge of the court of appeal   36 *gap and trade* opening and beaten path; *more preferments* additional high offices and honors   37 *the time* the unfolding course of events   43 *Incensed* stirred up and convinced   45 *pestilence* plague

46   That does infect the land; with which they moved
47   Have broken with the king, who hath so far
     Given ear to our complaint – of his great grace
49   And princely care, foreseeing those fell mischiefs
50   Our reasons laid before him – hath commanded
     Tomorrow morning to the council board
52   He be convented. He's a rank weed, Sir Thomas,
     And we must root him out. From your affairs
     I hinder you too long. Good night, Sir Thomas.

LOVELL

55   Many good nights, my lord. I rest your servant.

                              *Exeunt Gardiner and Page.*

     *Enter King and Suffolk.*

KING

     Charles, I will play no more tonight,
     My mind's not on't, you are too hard for me.

SUFFOLK

     Sir, I did never win of you before.

KING

     But little, Charles,
60   Nor shall not when my fancy's on my play.
     Now, Lovell, from the queen what is the news?

LOVELL

62   I could not personally deliver to her
     What you commanded me, but by her woman
     I sent your message, who returned her thanks
     In the great'st humbleness, and desired your highness
     Most heartily to pray for her.

KING                              What say'st thou? Ha?
     To pray for her? What, is she crying out?

LOVELL

68   So said her woman, and that her suff'rance made
     Almost each pang a death.

---

46 *moved* aroused   47 *broken with* conveyed their views to   49 *fell* deadly
50 *hath* that he has   52 *convented* summoned   55 *rest* remain   62 *deliver*
convey   68 *suff'rance* suffering

KING                                    Alas good lady.
SUFFOLK
  God safely quit her of her burden, and                          70
  With gentle travail, to the gladding of                         71
  Your highness with an heir.
KING                                'Tis midnight, Charles.
  Prithee to bed, and in thy prayers remember
  Th' estate of my poor queen. Leave me alone,                    74
  For I must think of that which company
  Would not be friendly to.
SUFFOLK                        I wish your highness
  A quiet night, and my good mistress will
  Remember in my prayers.
KING                            Charles, good night.
                                            *Exit Suffolk.*

    *Enter Sir Anthony Denny.*
  Well, sir, what follows?
DENNY
  Sir, I have brought my lord the archbishop                      80
  As you commanded me.
KING                            Ha? Canterbury?
DENNY
  Ay, my good lord.
KING                    'Tis true: where is he, Denny?
DENNY
  He attends your highness' pleasure.
KING                                    Bring him to us.
                                            *Exit Denny.*

LOVELL   *[Aside]*
  This is about that which the bishop spake.
  I am happily come hither.                                       85
    *Enter Cranmer and Denny.*
KING
  Avoid the gallery.                                              86

---

**70** *quit* release   **71** *gladding* making happy   **74** *estate* condition   **85** *happily*
fortunately   **86** *Avoid* leave

*[Lovell seems to stay.]*
                Ha! I have said. Be gone.
What!                  *Exeunt Lovell and Denny.*

CRANMER   *[Aside]*
          I am fearful. Wherefore frowns he thus?
88    'Tis his aspect of terror. All's not well.

KING
    How now, my lord? You do desire to know
90    Wherefore I sent for you?

CRANMER   *[Kneels.]*       It is my duty
    T' attend your highness' pleasure.

KING                     Pray you arise,
    My good and gracious Lord of Canterbury.
    Come, you and I must walk a turn together;
    I have news to tell you. Come, come give me your
      hand.
    Ah, my good lord, I grieve at what I speak
    And am right sorry to repeat what follows.
    I have, and most unwillingly, of late
    Heard many grievous – I do say, my lord,
    Grievous – complaints of you, which being considered,
100   Have moved us and our council, that you shall
    This morning come before us, where I know
102   You cannot with such freedom purge yourself
    But that, till further trial in those charges
    Which will require your answer, you must take
    Your patience to you, and be well contented
106   To make your house our Tower. You, a brother of us,
107   It fits we thus proceed, or else no witness
    Would come against you.

CRANMER   *[Kneels.]*      I humbly thank your highness,
    And am right glad to catch this good occasion

---

88 *aspect of terror* frightening expression  **100** *moved* prompted  **102** *freedom* i.e., comprehensive openness; *purge yourself* clear yourself of charges  **106** *brother of us* i.e., fellow councillor  **107** *fits* is fitting

Most throughly to be winnowed, where my chaff          110
And corn shall fly asunder. For I know
There's none stands under more calumnious tongues          112
Than I myself, poor man.

KING                                 Stand up, good Canterbury,
Thy truth and thy integrity is rooted
In us, thy friend. Give me thy hand, stand up;
  *[Cranmer rises.]*
Prithee let's walk. Now by my holidame,          116
What manner of man are you? My lord, I looked          117
You would have given me your petition, that
I should have ta'en some pains to bring together
Yourself and your accusers, and to have heard you          120
Without indurance further.          121

CRANMER                           Most dread liege,
The good I stand on is my truth and honesty.
If they shall fail, I with mine enemies          123
Will triumph o'er my person, which I weigh not,          124
Being of those virtues vacant. I fear nothing          125
What can be said against me.

KING                                   Know you not
How your state stands i' th' world, with the whole
  world?
Your enemies are many and not small; their practices          128
Must bear the same proportion, and not ever          129
The justice and the truth o' th' question carries          130
The due o' th' verdict with it. At what ease
Might corrupt minds procure knaves as corrupt
To swear against you! Such things have been done.
You are potently opposed, and with a malice

---

110 *throughly* thoroughly   112 *stands under* is subject to   116 *by my holidame* i.e., by our Lady   117 *looked* expected   121 *indurance further* further
hardship   123 *shall fail* prove lacking   124 *my person* i.e., my mere self;
*weigh not* don't value   125 *vacant* lacking   128 *practices* intrigues, plots
129 *bear . . . proportion* be of corresponding magnitude   130 *question*
cause   130–31 *carries . . . it* ensures the just verdict

135   Of as great size. Ween you of better luck,
136   I mean in perjured witness, than your Master,
     Whose minister you are, whiles here he lived
138   Upon this naughty earth? Go to, go to,
     You take a precipice for no leap of danger,
140   And woo your own destruction.

CRANMER              God and your majesty
     Protect mine innocence, or I fall into
     The trap is laid for me!

KING              Be of good cheer,
143   They shall no more prevail than we give way to.
     Keep comfort to you, and this morning see
145   You do appear before them. If they shall chance
146   In charging you with matters to commit you,
     The best persuasions to the contrary
     Fail not to use, and with what vehemency
     Th' occasion shall instruct you. If entreaties
150   Will render you no remedy, this ring
     Deliver them, and your appeal to us
     There make before them. Look, the good man weeps:
     He's honest on mine honor! God's blessed mother,
     I swear he is truehearted, and a soul
     None better in my kingdom. Get you gone
     And do as I have bid you.     *[Exit Cranmer.]*
               He has strangled
     His language in his tears.
      *Enter Old Lady.*

GENTLEMAN   *[Within]*   Come back: what mean you?
OLD LADY
     I'll not come back. The tidings that I bring
     Will make my boldness manners. Now good angels
160   Fly o'er thy royal head and shade thy person
     Under their blessed wings!

---

**135** *Ween you of* do you imagine **136** *witness* evidence **138** *naughty* wicked **143** *give way to* allow them scope **145–46** *chance . . . charging you* venture to charge you **146** *commit* i.e., to the prison of the Tower

KING                              Now by thy looks
  I guess thy message. Is the queen delivered?
  Say ay, and of a boy.
OLD LADY                    Ay, ay, my liege,
  And of a lovely boy. The God of heaven
  Both now and ever bless her: 'tis a girl
  Promises boys hereafter. Sir, your queen
  Desires your visitation, and to be                              167
  Acquainted with this stranger. 'Tis as like you
  As cherry is to cherry.
KING                          Lovell!
    *[Enter Lovell.]*
LOVELL                          Sir?
KING
  Give her an hundred marks. I'll to the queen.          170
                                *Exit King.*

OLD LADY
  An hundred marks? By this light, I'll ha' more!
  An ordinary groom is for such payment.
  I will have more or scold it out of him.
  Said I for this the girl was like to him?
  I'll have more or else unsay't; and now, while 'tis hot,
  I'll put it to the issue.          *Exit Lady [with Lovell].*   176

*

❧ **V.2**   *Enter Cranmer, Archbishop of Canterbury*
    *[; Pursuivants, Pages, and Footboys at the door].*


CRANMER
  I hope I am not too late, and yet the gentleman
  That was sent to me from the council prayed me
  To make great haste. All fast? What means this? Ho!          3

---

**167** *visitation* visit   **170** *an hundred marks* (£66, a substantial sum, despite
the old lady's disgruntled response)   **176** *put . . . issue* bring it to a head
    **V.2** Outside the council chamber **s.d.** *Pursuivants* junior officers of the
state   **3** *fast* shut (i.e., the doors)

Who waits there? Sure you know me?
   *Enter Keeper.*

KEEPER                                      Yes, my lord.
But yet I cannot help you.

CRANMER
  Why?

KEEPER
Your grace must wait till you be called for.
   *Enter Doctor Butts.*

CRANMER                                  So.

BUTTS   *[Aside]*
This is a piece of malice. I am glad

9  I came this way so happily. The king

10  Shall understand it presently.             *Exit.*

CRANMER                 'Tis Butts,
The king's physician. As he passed along,
How earnestly he cast his eyes upon me.

13  Pray heaven he sound not my disgrace, for certain

14  This is of purpose laid by some that hate me
(God turn their hearts, I never sought their malice)
To quench mine honor. They would shame to make me
Wait else at door, a fellow councillor,
'Mong boys, grooms, and lackeys. But their pleasures

19  Must be fulfilled, and I attend with patience.
   *Enter the King and Butts at a window above.*

BUTTS

20  I'll show your grace the strangest sight –

KING                            What's that, Butts?

BUTTS
I think your highness saw this many a day.

KING

22  Body a me; where is it?

BUTTS                  There, my lord:

---

9 *happily* fortunately   10 *presently* at once   13 *sound* make known   14 *laid* prepared as a trap   19 s.d. (note use of upper stage, not called for elsewhere in the play)   22 *Body a me* (exclamation, "by my body")

The high promotion of his grace of Canterbury,
Who holds his state at door 'mongst pursuivants,        24
Pages, and footboys.
KING                        Ha? 'Tis he indeed.
Is this the honor they do one another?
'Tis well there's one above 'em yet. I had thought       27
They had parted so much honesty among 'em –             28
At least good manners – as not thus to suffer
A man of his place and so near our favor               30
To dance attendance on their lordships' pleasures,
And at the door too, like a post with packets.          32
By holy Mary, Butts, there's knavery!
Let 'em alone, and draw the curtain close.             34
We shall hear more anon.                               35
    *A council table brought in with chairs and stools, and*
    *placed under the state. Enter Lord Chancellor, places*
    *himself at the upper end of the table on the left hand, a*
    *seat being left void above him, as for Canterbury's seat.*
    *Duke of Suffolk, Duke of Norfolk, Surrey, Lord*
    *Chamberlain, Gardiner seat themselves in order on*
    *each side. Cromwell at lower end, as secretary.*
CHANCELLOR
Speak to the business, master secretary.
Why are we met in council?
CROMWELL                        Please your honors,
The chief cause concerns his grace of Canterbury.
GARDINER
Has he had knowledge of it?                            39
CROMWELL                        Yes.
NORFOLK                                Who waits there?
KEEPER
Without, my noble lords?                               40

---

24 *holds his state* maintains his dignity   27 *one above* (1) Henry (?), (2) God
(?)   28 *parted* shared; *honesty* decency   30 *place* rank   32 *post* courier; *pack-*
*ets* mail   34 *Let 'em alone* don't disturb them   35 s.d. *state* chair of state   39
*had knowledge* been informed   40 *Without* outside

**GARDINER**                              Yes.

**KEEPER**                                      My lord archbishop,
   And has done half an hour to know your pleasures.

**CHANCELLOR**
   Let him come in.

**KEEPER**                    Your grace may enter now.
   *Cranmer approaches the council table.*

**CHANCELLOR**
   My good lord archbishop, I'm very sorry

44  To sit here at this present and behold
   That chair stand empty; but we are all men

46  In our own natures frail, and capable
   Of our flesh; few are angels; out of which frailty
   And want of wisdom, you, that best should teach us,

49  Have misdemeaned yourself, and not a little:

50  Toward the king first, then his laws, in filling
   The whole realm by your teaching and your chaplains'
   (For so we are informed) with new opinions,

53  Divers and dangerous, which are heresies,

54  And not reformed may prove pernicious.

**GARDINER**
   Which reformation must be sudden too,
   My noble lords; for those that tame wild horses
   Pace 'em not in their hands to make 'em gentle,

58  But stop their mouths with stubborn bits and spur 'em

59  Till they obey the manage. If we suffer,

60  Out of our easiness and childish pity
   To one man's honor, this contagious sickness,
   Farewell all physic! And what follows then?

63  Commotions, uproars, with a general taint
   Of the whole state, as of late days our neighbors,

65  The upper Germany, can dearly witness,

---

44 *at this present* right now   46–47 *capable . . . flesh* prone to the weaknesses
of the flesh   49 *misdemeaned yourself* conducted yourself improperly   53
*Divers* various, heterodox   54 *pernicious* extremely harmful   58 *stubborn*
hard   59 *manage* handling (here, rider's control)   60 *easiness* indulgence,
laxity   63 *taint* corruption   65 *upper* i.e., interior

Yet freshly pitied in our memories.

CRANMER
My good lords, hitherto, in all the progress
Both of my life and office, I have labored,
And with no little study, that my teaching                69
And the strong course of my authority                     70
Might go one way, and safely, and the end
Was ever to do well; nor is there living
(I speak it with a single heart, my lords)                73
A man that more detests, more stirs against,              74
Both in his private conscience and his place,             75
Defacers of a public peace than I do.                     76
Pray heaven the king may never find a heart
With less allegiance in it! Men that make
Envy and crookèd malice nourishment
Dare bite the best. I do beseech your lordships           80
That in this case of justice, my accusers,
Be what they will, may stand forth face to face           82
And freely urge against me.                               83

SUFFOLK                         Nay, my lord,
That cannot be. You are a councillor,
And by that virtue no man dare accuse you.                85

GARDINER
My lord, because we have business of more moment,         86
We will be short with you. 'Tis his highness' pleasure
And our consent, for better trial of you,
From hence you be committed to the Tower,
Where, being but a private man again,                     90
You shall know many dare accuse you boldly,
More than, I fear, you are provided for.

CRANMER
Ah, my good Lord of Winchester, I thank you;

---

**69** *study* effort, pains   **73** *single* undivided   **74** *stirs* takes action   **75** *place*
office   **76** *Defacers* destroyers   **82** *Be what they will* whoever they may be
**83** *urge* press their charges   **85** *by that virtue* by virtue of that   **86** *moment*
importance

You are always my good friend. If your will pass,
I shall both find your lordship judge and juror,
You are so merciful. I see your end:
'Tis my undoing. Love and meekness, lord,
Become a churchman better than ambition;
99    Win straying souls with modesty again,
100   Cast none away. That I shall clear myself,
101   Lay all the weight ye can upon my patience,
102   I make as little doubt as you do conscience
In doing daily wrongs. I could say more, ·
But reverence to your calling makes me modest.

GARDINER
105   My lord, my lord, you are a sectary,
106   That's the plain truth. Your painted gloss discovers,
107   To men that understand you, words and weakness.

CROMWELL
My lord of Winchester, you're a little,
By your good favor, too sharp. Men so noble,
110   However faulty, yet should find respect
For what they have been. 'Tis a cruelty
To load a falling man.

GARDINER                    Good master secretary,
113   I cry your honor mercy. You may worst
Of all this table say so.

CROMWELL                    Why, my lord?

GARDINER
Do not I know you for a favorer
116   Of this new sect? Ye are not sound.

CROMWELL                              Not sound?

GARDINER
Not sound, I say.

CROMWELL                Would you were half so honest!

---

99 *modesty* moderation   101 *Lay . . . can* exert all the pressure you can   102
*I make . . . conscience* I have as little doubt as you have scruple   105 *sectary*
adherent of a heretical sect   106 *painted gloss* specious rhetoric; *discovers* re-
veals   107 *words* mere words   110 *find* meet with   113 *I cry . . . mercy* I
beg your honor's pardon; *worst* with least cause   116 *sound* loyal

Men's prayers then would seek you, not their fears.
GARDINER
I shall remember this bold language.
CROMWELL                              Do.
Remember your bold life too.                                        120
CHANCELLOR                    That is too much.
Forbear for shame, my lords.
GARDINER                    I have done.
CROMWELL                                    And I.
CHANCELLOR
Then thus for you, my lord: it stands agreed,
I take it, by all voices, that forthwith                           123
You be conveyed to th' Tower a prisoner,                           124
There to remain till the king's further pleasure
Be known unto us. Are you all agreed, lords?
ALL
We are.
CRANMER    Is there no other way of mercy
But I must needs to th' Tower, my lords?
GARDINER                                    What other
Would you expect? You are strangely troublesome.                  129
Let some o' th' guard be ready there!                             130
    *Enter the Guard.*
CRANMER                              For me?
Must I go like a traitor thither?                                  131
GARDINER                    Receive him
And see him safe i' th' Tower.
CRANMER                    Stay, good my lords,
I have a little yet to say. Look there, my lords.
By virtue of that ring I take my cause
Out of the gripes of cruel men and give it                        135
To a most noble judge, the king my master.
CHAMBERLAIN
This is the king's ring.

---

123 *voices* votes   124 *conveyed* escorted   129 *strangely* extraordinarily   131
*Receive* take   135 *gripes* clutches

SURREY               'Tis no counterfeit.

SUFFOLK
'Tis the right ring, by heav'n! I told ye all,
When we first put this dangerous stone a-rolling,
140   'Twould fall upon ourselves.

NORFOLK           Do you think, my lords,
The king will suffer but the little finger
Of this man to be vexed?

CHAMBERLAIN         'Tis now too certain,
143   How much more is his life in value with him.
144   Would I were fairly out on't!

CROMWELL         My mind gave me,
145   In seeking tales and informations
Against this man, whose honesty the devil
And his disciples only envy at,
148   Ye blew the fire that burns ye: now have at ye!

*Enter King, frowning on them; takes his seat.*

GARDINER
Dread sovereign, how much are we bound to heaven
150   In daily thanks, that gave us such a prince,
Not only good and wise but most religious;
One that in all obedience makes the church
The chief aim of his honor, and to strengthen
154   That holy duty out of dear respect,
His royal self in judgment comes to hear
The cause betwixt her and this great offender.

KING
157   You were ever good at sudden commendations,
Bishop of Winchester. But know I come not
To hear such flattery now, and in my presence
160   They are too thin and base to hide offenses;
To me you cannot reach. You play the spaniel,
And think with wagging of your tongue to win me.

---

143 *in value* esteemed   144 *My . . . me* I had a misgiving   145 *tales and informations* incriminating hearsay   148 *have at ye* look out for yourselves
154 *dear* heartfelt   157 *sudden commendations* impromptu compliments

But whatsoe'er thou tak'st me for, I'm sure
Thou hast a cruel nature and a bloody.
  *[To Cranmer]*
Good man, sit down. Now let me see the proudest
He, that dares most, but wag his finger at thee.                    166
By all that's holy, he had better starve                            167
Than but once think his place becomes thee not.

SURREY
  May it please your grace –

KING                                     No, sir, it does not please me.
I had thought I had had men of some understanding     *170*
And wisdom of my council; but I find none.
Was it discretion, lords, to let this man,
This good man (few of you deserve that title),
This honest man, wait like a lousy footboy              174
At chamber door? And one as great as you are?
Why, what a shame was this? Did my commission          176
Bid ye so far forget yourselves? I gave ye
Power as he was a councillor to try him,
Not as a groom. There's some of ye, I see,
More out of malice than integrity,                     *180*
Would try him to the utmost, had ye mean,               181
Which ye shall never have while I live.

CHANCELLOR                                    Thus far,
My most dread sovereign, may it like your grace        183
To let my tongue excuse all. What was purposed
Concerning his imprisonment was rather
(If there be faith in men) meant for his trial
And fair purgation to the world than malice,           187
I'm sure, in me.

KING                    Well, well, my lords, respect him.
Take him, and use him well; he's worthy of it.
I will say thus much for him: if a prince               *190*

---

166 *He* man   167 *starve* die   174 *lousy* covered with lice   176 *shame* inflic-
tion of dishonor   181 *try* harass, afflict   183 *like* please   187 *purgation*
clearing of himself

191      May be beholding to a subject, I
         Am for his love and service so to him.
         Make me no more ado, but all embrace him.
         Be friends for shame, my lords. My Lord of Canter-
            bury,
         I have a suit which you must not deny me;
         That is, a fair young maid that yet wants baptism,
         You must be godfather and answer for her.

CRANMER
         The greatest monarch now alive may glory
         In such an honor. How may I deserve it
200      That am a poor and humble subject to you?

201  KING    Come, come, my lord, you'd spare your spoons!
202      You shall have two noble partners with you, the old
         Duchess of Norfolk and Lady Marquis Dorset. Will
         these please you?
         Once more, my Lord of Winchester, I charge you
         Embrace and love this man.

GARDINER                          With a true heart
207      And brother love I do it.

CRANMER                          And let heaven
         Witness how dear I hold this confirmation.

KING
         Good man, those joyful tears show thy true heart.
210      The common voice I see is verified
         Of thee, which says thus: "Do my Lord of Canterbury
212      A shrewd turn, and he's your friend for ever."
         Come, lords, we trifle time away. I long
         To have this young one made a Christian.
         As I have made ye one, lords, one remain;
         So I grow stronger, you more honor gain.        *Exeunt.*

                              *

---

191 *beholding* indebted   201 *you'd ... spoons* i.e., you'd economize by not
giving the traditional apostle spoons to godchildren (Henry is teasing Cranmer)   202 *partners* i.e., fellow godparents   207 *brother love* brotherly love
212 *shrewd* bad

∾ **V.3** *Noise and tumult within. Enter Porter and his*
*Man.*

PORTER   You'll leave your noise anon, ye rascals! Do you
 take the court for Parish Garden? Ye rude slaves, leave   2
 your gaping!   3
[ONE]   *Within*   Good master porter, I belong to th' larder.   4
PORTER   Belong to th' gallows and be hanged, ye rogue!
 Is this a place to roar in? Fetch me a dozen crab-tree
 staves, and strong ones; these are but switches to 'em:   7
 I'll scratch your heads. You must be seeing christenings?
 Do you look for ale and cakes here, you rude rascals?   9
MAN
 Pray, sir, be patient; 'tis as much impossible,   10
 Unless we sweep 'em from the door with cannons,
 To scatter 'em as 'tis to make 'em sleep
 On May Day morning, which will never be.   13
 We may as well push against Paul's as stir 'em.   14
PORTER   How got they in, and be hanged?
MAN
 Alas I know not, how gets the tide in!
 As much as one sound cudgel of four foot
 (You see the poor remainder) could distribute,
 I made no spare, sir.   19
PORTER       You did nothing, sir.
MAN
 I am not Samson, nor Sir Guy, nor Colebrand,   20
 To mow 'em down before me. But if I spared any
 That had a head to hit, either young or old,
 He or she, cuckold or cuckold maker,

---

**V.3** The palace courtyard   **2** *Parish Garden* Paris Garden (a London venue
for cruel, unruly sports like bearbaiting and bullbaiting)   **3** *gaping* bawling
**4** *belong to* i.e., am employed in   **7** *switches* thin canes   **9** *ale and cakes* (traditional festive fare)   **13** *May Day* May 1 (traditionally, a day of festivity)
**14** *Paul's* Saint Paul's Cathedral   **19** *made no spare* didn't stint   **20**
*Samson . . . Colebrand* (Samson, Guy of Warwick, and Colebrand – a giant
slain by Guy in a popular story – were all noted for great strength)

24    Let me ne'er hope to see a chine again,
25    And that I would not for a cow, God save her.
[ONE] *Within* Do you hear, master porter?
PORTER  I shall be with you presently, good master
    puppy. Keep the door close, sirrah.
MAN  What would you have me do?
30  PORTER  What should you do but knock 'em down by
31    th' dozens? Is this Moorfields to muster in? Or have we
32    some strange Indian with the great tool come to court,
33    the women so besiege us? Bless me, what a fry of forni-
    cation is at door! On my Christian conscience this one
    christening will beget a thousand; here will be father,
    godfather, and all together.
37  MAN  The spoons will be the bigger, sir. There is a fellow
38    somewhat near the door, he should be a brazier by his
39    face, for o' my conscience twenty of the dog days now
40    reign in's nose. All that stand about him are under the
41    line; they need no other penance. That firedrake did I
    hit three times on the head, and three times was his
43    nose discharged against me; he stands there like a mor-
44    tar piece to blow us. There was a haberdasher's wife of
45    small wit near him, that railed upon me till her pinked
    porringer fell off her head, for kindling such a combus-
    tion in the state. I missed the meteor once and hit that
48    woman, who cried out "Clubs," when I might see from

---

24 *chine* joint of beef   25 *not for a cow* (common expression, meaning "not for anything")   31 *Moorfields* (a park where military training was conducted); *muster* assemble (as for military training)   32 *strange Indian . . . tool* (North American Indian, already apparently the subject of European legends or fantasies regarding extraordinary penis size)   33–34 *fry of fornication* swarm of would-be fornicators   37 *spoons* i.e., christening spoons (cf. V.2.201)   38 *brazier* brass maker   39 *dog days* i.e., hottest season (July 13–August 15), when the Dog Star, Sirius, rises at the same time as the sun   40 *reign in's nose* i.e., his nose has a fiery red glow   41 *line* equator; *firedrake* meteor (still referring to the red nose)   43 *discharged* fired (like a cannon)   43–44 *like a mortar piece* i.e., gaping upward   44 *blow us* blow us up; *haberdasher* purveyor of small garments, ribbons, etc.   45–46 *pinked porringer* round cap ornamented with perforations, looking like a porridge dish   48 *Clubs* (the call that summoned apprentices to start or stop a fight)

far some forty truncheoners draw to her succor, which    49
were the hope o' th' Strond, where she was quartered.    50
They fell on, I made good my place. At length they       51
came to th' broomstaff to me; I defied 'em still, when    52
suddenly a file of boys behind 'em, loose shot, delivered    53
such a shower of pebbles that I was fain to draw mine    54
honor in and let 'em win the work. The devil was          55
amongst 'em I think surely.

PORTER   These are the youths that thunder at a playhouse and fight for bitten apples, that no audience but
the tribulation of Tower Hill or the limbs of Lime-       59
house, their dear brothers, are able to endure. I have    60
some of 'em in Limbo Patrum, and there they are like      61
to dance these three days, besides the running banquet    62
of two beadles that is to come.
   *Enter Lord Chamberlain.*

CHAMBERLAIN
Mercy o' me, what a multitude are here!
They grow still too; from all parts they are coming
As if we kept a fair here. Where are these porters,
These lazy knaves? Y' have made a fine hand, fellows!    67
There's a trim rabble let in; are all these              68
Your faithful friends o' th' suburbs? We shall have      69
Great store of room, no doubt, left for the ladies       70
When they pass back from the christening.                71
PORTER                                   An't please
   your honor,

---

**49** *truncheoners* cudgel bearers  **50** *Strond* Strand (a fashionable street in London)  **51** *fell on* attacked; *made good my place* held my ground  **52** *broomstaff* i.e., close quarters  **53** *loose shot* marksmen not attached to a company  **54** *fain* obliged  **55** *work* fortification  **59** *tribulation of Tower Hill* (a particular gang of ruffians) (?); *limbs* youths (*of Limehouse* possibly referring to another youth gang)  **61** *Limbo Patrum* prison (refers to a region near hell in traditional Catholic belief)  **62–63** *running . . . beadles* i.e., whipping by public officials known as beadles, the offender being forced to run through the streets while being whipped  **67** *made a fine hand* done a nice job (ironic)  **68** *trim* elegant (ironic)  **69** *suburbs* areas outside city jurisdiction  **71** *An't* if it

We are but men, and what so many may do,
Not being torn apieces, we have done.
74     An army cannot rule 'em.

CHAMBERLAIN                              As I live,
75     If the king blame me for't, I'll lay ye all
76     By th' heels, and suddenly; and on your heads
77     Clap round fines for neglect. You're lazy knaves,
78     And here ye lie baiting of bombards when
       Ye should do service. Hark, the trumpets sound!
80     Th' are come already from the christening.
81     Go break among the press, and find a way out
82     To let the troop pass fairly, or I'll find
83     A Marshalsea shall hold ye play these two months.

PORTER
       Make way there for the princess!

MAN                                     You great fellow,
85     Stand close up, or I'll make your head ache!

PORTER
86     You i' th' chamblet, get up o' th' rail,
87     I'll peck you o'er the pales else!              *Exeunt.*

                              *

∾ **V.4** *Enter Trumpets, sounding; then two Aldermen,
       Lord Mayor, Garter, Cranmer, Duke of Norfolk with
       his marshal's staff, Duke of Suffolk, two Noblemen
       bearing great standing bowls for the christening gifts;
       then four Noblemen bearing a canopy, under which
       the Duchess of Norfolk, godmother, bearing the child
       richly habited in a mantle, etc., train borne by a Lady;*

---

74 *rule* control   75–76 *lay . . . heels* clap you in the stocks   76 *suddenly* immediately   77 *Clap* impose; *round* heavy   78 *baiting of bombards* drinking deep (out of leathern bottles)   81 *among the press* through the crowd   82 *fairly* in orderly fashion   83 *Marshalsea* prison in Southwark   85 *close up* out of the way   86 *chamblet* camlet (a rich fabric made of goat's hair)   87 *peck you . . . pales* pitch you over the rails (barricades)
   **V.4** The palace   **s.d.** *Trumpets* trumpeters; *Garter* (see note on IV.1.36, item 5); *standing bowls* bowls with legs; *habited* garbed

*then follows the Marchioness Dorset, the other god-*
*mother, and Ladies. The troop pass once about the*
*stage, and Garter speaks.*

GARTER    Heaven, from thy endless goodness, send pros-    1
perous life, long and ever happy, to the high and
mighty princess of England, Elizabeth.
    *Flourish. Enter King and Guard.*
CRANMER    *[Kneels.]*
And to your royal grace and the good queen,
My noble partners and myself thus pray                    5
All comfort, joy in this most gracious lady,
Heaven ever laid up to make parents happy,
May hourly fall upon ye!
KING                        Thank you, good lord arch-
bishop.
What is her name?
CRANMER            Elizabeth.
KING                        Stand up, lord.
    *[Cranmer rises. The King kisses the child.]*
With this kiss take my blessing. God protect thee,    10
Into whose hand I give thy life.
CRANMER                        Amen.
KING
My noble gossips, y' have been too prodigal;          12
I thank ye heartily. So shall this lady,
When she has so much English.
CRANMER                        Let me speak, sir,
For heaven now bids me, and the words I utter
Let none think flattery, for they'll find 'em truth.
This royal infant – heaven still move about her! –    17
Though in her cradle, yet now promises
Upon this land a thousand thousand blessings,

---

1–3 *Heaven . . . Elizabeth* (a formula used on such occasions)   5 *partners* fellow godparents   12 *gossips* godparents; *prodigal* generous   17 *heaven . . .*
*her* may God be always near her

20    Which time shall bring to ripeness. She shall be
      (But few now living can behold that goodness)
      A pattern to all princes living with her
23    And all that shall succeed. Saba was never
      More covetous of wisdom and fair virtue
      Than this pure soul shall be. All princely graces
26    That mold up such a mighty piece as this is,
      With all the virtues that attend the good,
      Shall still be doubled on her. Truth shall nurse her,
29    Holy and heavenly thoughts still counsel her;
30    She shall be loved and feared; her own shall bless her;
      Her foes shake like a field of beaten corn
      And hang their heads with sorrow. Good grows with
          her;
      In her days every man shall eat in safety
      Under his own vine what he plants, and sing
      The merry songs of peace to all his neighbors.
      God shall be truly known, and those about her
37    From her shall read the perfect ways of honor,
      And by those claim their greatness, not by blood.
      Nor shall this peace sleep with her, but as when
40    The bird of wonder dies, the maiden phoenix,
41    Her ashes new create another heir
42    As great in admiration as herself,
      So shall she leave her blessedness to one
44    (When heaven shall call her from this cloud of dark-
          ness)
      Who from the sacred ashes of her honor
      Shall starlike rise, as great in fame as she was,

---

23 *Saba* biblical Queen of Sheba, who visited Solomon on account of his reputed wisdom   26 *mold . . . piece* constitute so great a work (person)   29
*still* always   30 *own* own people   37 *read* learn   40 *maiden phoenix* (Elizabeth had often been compared to the mythical, self-regenerating phoenix)
41 *heir* (James I, the reigning monarch at the time *Henry VIII* was written,
inheriting from Elizabeth, but not as the natural offspring of the queen, who
died unmarried)   42 *As great in admiration* i.e., just as wondrous   44 *cloud
of darkness* i.e., this dark, mortal condition

And so stand fixed. Peace, plenty, love, truth, terror,
That were the servants to this chosen infant,
Shall then be his, and like a vine grow to him.
Wherever the bright sun of heaven shall shine,                    *50*
His honor and the greatness of his name
Shall be, and make new nations. He shall flourish
And like a mountain cedar reach his branches
To all the plains about him. Our children's children
Shall see this, and bless heaven.

KING                                        Thou speakest wonders.

CRANMER
She shall be, to the happiness of England,
An aged princess; many days shall see her,
And yet no day without a deed to crown it.
Would I had known no more! But she must die –
She must, the saints must have her – yet a virgin.               *60*
A most unspotted lily shall she pass
To th' ground, and all the world shall mourn her.

KING
O lord archbishop,
Thou hast made me now a man. Never before                        *64*
This happy child did I get anything.                             *65*
This oracle of comfort has so pleased me
That when I am in heaven I shall desire
To see what this child does, and praise my Maker.
I thank ye all. To you, my good lord mayor,
And you good brethren, I am much beholding.                      *70*
I have received much honor by your presence,
And ye shall find me thankful. Lead the way, lords,
Ye must all see the queen, and she must thank ye;
She will be sick else. This day, no man think                   *74*
'Has business at his house, for all shall stay:                 *75*
This little one shall make it Holy Day.            *Exeunt.*

※

---

64 *a man* i.e., a happy, thriving man   65 *get* beget   70 *beholding* indebted
74 *sick* unhappy   75 *'Has* i.e., he has

## THE EPILOGUE

❧ **Epi.**

'Tis ten to one this play can never please
All that are here. Some come to take their ease
And sleep an act or two, but those we fear
W' have frighted with our trumpets, so 'tis clear
5    They'll say 'tis naught; others to hear the city
Abused extremely, and to cry "That's witty,"
7    Which we have not done neither; that I fear
All the expected good w' are like to hear
For this play at this time, is only in
10    The merciful construction of good women,
For such a one we showed 'em. If they smile
And say 'twill do, I know within a while
13    All the best men are ours; for 'tis ill hap,
14    If they hold when their ladies bid 'em clap.

---

**Epilogue**   **5** *naught* bad   **7** *that* so that   **10** *construction* interpretation   **13**
*ill hap* an unhappy circumstance   **14** *hold* hold back

The distinguished Pelican Shakespeare series, newly revised
to be the premier choice for students, professors, and
general readers well into the 21st century

# FOR THE BEST IN PAPERBACKS, LOOK FOR THE

In every corner of the world, on every subject under the sun, Penguin represents quality and variety—the very best in publishing today.

For complete information about books available from Penguin—including Puffins, Penguin Classics, and Compass—and how to order them, write to us at the appropriate address below. Please note that for copyright reasons the selection of books varies from country to country.

**In the United Kingdom:** Please write to *Dept. EP, Penguin Books Ltd, Bath Road, Harmondsworth, West Drayton, Middlesex UB7 0DA.*

**In the United States:** Please write to *Penguin Putnam Inc., P.O. Box 12289 Dept. B, Newark, New Jersey 07101-5289* or call 1-800-788-6262.

**In Canada:** Please write to *Penguin Books Canada Ltd, 10 Alcorn Avenue, Suite 300, Toronto, Ontario M4V 3B2.*

**In Australia:** Please write to *Penguin Books Australia Ltd, P.O. Box 257, Ringwood, Victoria 3134.*

**In New Zealand:** Please write to *Penguin Books (NZ) Ltd, Private Bag 102902, North Shore Mail Centre, Auckland 10.*

**In India:** Please write to *Penguin Books India Pvt Ltd, 11 Panchsheel Shopping Centre, Panchsheel Park, New Delhi 110 017.*

**In the Netherlands:** Please write to *Penguin Books Netherlands bv, Postbus 3507, NL-1001 AH Amsterdam.*

**In Germany:** Please write to *Penguin Books Deutschland GmbH, Metzlerstrasse 26, 60594 Frankfurt am Main.*

**In Spain:** Please write to *Penguin Books S. A., Bravo Murillo 19, 1° B, 28015 Madrid.*

**In Italy:** Please write to *Penguin Italia s.r.l., Via Benedetto Croce 2, 20094 Corsico, Milano.*

**In France:** Please write to *Penguin France, Le Carré Wilson, 62 rue Benjamin Baillaud, 31500 Toulouse.*

**In Japan:** Please write to *Penguin Books Japan Ltd, Kaneko Building, 2-3-25 Koraku, Bunkyo-Ku, Tokyo 112.*

**In South Africa:** Please write to *Penguin Books South Africa (Pty) Ltd, Private Bag X14, Parkview, 2122 Johannesburg.*